THE TOTAL CAT

The TOTAL CAT

**Understanding Your Cat's
Physical and Emotional
Behavior from Kitten
to Old Age**

Carole C. Wilbourn
The Cat Therapist

Quill

A HarperResource Book

An Imprint of HarperCollinsPublishers

HarperCollins books may be purchased for educational, business, or sales promotional use. For information please write: Special Markets Department, HarperCollins Publishers Inc., 10 East 53rd Street, New York, New York 10022-5299.

FIRST EDITION 2000

Library of Congress Cataloging in Publication Data:
Wilbourn, Carole, 1940–
  The total cat: understanding your cat's physical and emotional behavior from kitten to old age / by Carole Wilbourn.—1st ed.
    p. cm.
  ISBN 0-380-79051-3
  1. Cats. 2. Cats—Behavior. I. Title.
SF442.W483 2000
636.8'0887—dc21   00-040846

01 02 03 04   RRD 10 9 8 7 6 5 4 3

The author, a Cat Therapist, has written this book as a tutorial and source of information. It is based on her three decades of research, experience, and personal observations. With respect to any medical information contained herein, the author encourages consultation with a licensed veterinarian.

In loving memory of Oliver, my very first cat, who opened my heart to the absolute, honest, unqualified love of the cat. To Sambo, Muggsy, Muggsy-Baggins and Honey-Blue, who continued to nurture my being. For Sunny-Blue, my late domestic companion and media-mate, who adorns the cover of my book *Cat Talk*, whose many ways and spirit live on in his protege, Ziggy-Star-Dust.

For Ziggy-Star-Dust and Diana-Moon-Dust, my present companions, who inspire and nourish my soul.

On behalf of all my patients and to those cats who are in need.

Acknowledgments

To Phyllis Levy, who believed this book must be.

To my agent, Stephany Evans, who is all an agent should be.

To Sarah Durand, my editor, for her constant support and guidance.

To Ed Frascino, my illustrator, whose remarkable cartoons celebrate and capture *The Total Cat*.

With heartfelt thanks to my siblings and their spouses for their enduring love and faith.

Contents

Foreword

Carole Wilbourn knows cats. From the early 1970s, when she cofounded a cats-only veterinary hospital, to her thriving house-call practice of today, Carole has helped thousands of cats—and their people—through behavior lapses, health problems, and lifestyle changes. Her abiding love for the feline species has fueled a successful career spanning nearly three decades and encompassing everything from consultations, speeches at cat shows and cat behavior classes to numerous writings, including this book.

Few people are lucky enough, motivated enough, and talented enough to pursue a career that revolves around one of their passions. Carole's inspiration and singular gift for working with cats shine through in the energy and enthusiasm she devotes to all her activities. Her passion for these most mystical, wonderful creatures infuses every word, gesture, and touch.

I have worked with Carole since 1988, when I joined the staff of *Cat Fancy*. Carole has written the monthly magazine's "Cats on the Couch" column since 1984. Consistently ranking as one of the most popular columns in the magazine, "Cats on the Couch" is a reflection of Carole herself: warm, friendly, funny, knowledgeable, and unique. I have always been impressed at how closely *Cat Fancy* readers identify with Carole and the stories she relates. The column and Carole's books speak to ailurophiles at a level they can understand and with information they can use every day in living with cats.

As you read this book, you'll no doubt find yourself amused, amazed, heartened, and intrigued. And hopefully you'll begin to regard your feline friend with fresh insight, understanding, admiration, and love. If the book offers you just one new glimpse into the mind and magic of your cat—and I'm sure you'll glean many more—you, like many other cat lovers, will be able to thank Carole for enriching your relationship with your favorite furry companion.

Debbie Phillips-Donaldson,
Consulting Editorial Director,
Cat Fancy magazine

"I wish I could be certain of exactly what she expects of us."

Introduction

I hope that this book will help enhance your relationship with your cat. Throughout my twenty-five years in preventing and correcting cats' behavioral and emotional problems, I have devised the "Wilbourn ways." They have evolved from my work with veterinarians. In order to recognize and treat the "total" cat, a cat's physiological and emotional needs must be met to maintain a healthy cat.

My cat practice is a culmination of what I have learned from my early observations and interactions with cats when I was an ardent animal activist in the early sixties. When my sister Gail asked me in 1969 what I would ask for if I could have whatever career I wanted, I answered, "I want to help cats." A few months later I met Paul Rowan, a veterinarian, when he treated a sick cat I had adopted from a restaurant. Paul and cats became the two constant passions in my life.

I had my first "professional" experience when we lived in Malibu and opened an emergency veterinary service in

North Hollywood. Two years later, when we returned to New York, I took my postgraduate courses in psychology. But much of my time I observed cats' behavior. From their actions I deduced and interpreted their emotions. I concluded that if a cat's emotions were well balanced, so was his behavior. Conversely, if he felt bad, he would have behavioral problems.

In 1973, Paul and I opened the Cat Practice in Manhattan's West Village. It was the first veterinary hospital in New York that was devoted exclusively to cats. I had no definite idea where my path would lead, other than that I had an overwhelming passion for cats and a desire to help and nurture them. My initial role was as nurse, assistant, and office manager. But my observations and feelings about a patient became very important in making the medical diagnosis. Because of my psychological and secondary school teaching background, I naturally spoke to the clients personally and began to see feline patients who suffered only from emotional problems.

During our five years at the practice I was able to train a staff of twenty part-time students, who were primarily females from New York University (my alma mater), a senior citizen, a recovery nurse, and a few children whom I dubbed Les Jeunes Filles Auxiliary. I also wrote three books on cat behavior and a children's play in which Cary Grant, a reformed attack cat, was the star. Cary was the catalyst for the development of my method of treating a neurotic, aggressive cat.

In 1978 we concluded our pioneering work and sold the Cat Practice to Dr. William (Skip) Sullivan. At that time I started to make house calls and increased my telephone and letter consultation service. Media coverage of my work at the Cat Practice had been large and continued to grow. I continue to work with Dr. Sullivan and his associate, Dr. Kevin Shimmel, on behavioral cases.

My cat Sam passed on in 1979 at the age of sixteen.

Sam had lived with me longer than anyone. He had been a major influence in the writing of my three books. His photo adorned all my book jackets. Muggsy-Baggins, his nine-year-old friend, died a year later. I loved them dearly, so it was a time of grief. Two years later, Paul and I parted after twelve long and tumultuous years. It was then that I had the time and inclination to actively increase my house-call practice.

In 1984 I was asked to write a monthly column for *Cat Fancy* magazine, a significant vehicle for my advice on cat behavior and a continuous source of personal pleasure.

Many of my case referrals were from veterinarians, the first of whom were Drs. Paul Cavanagh and Ann Lucas. Dr. Cavanagh, a good friend who had worked with us at the practice, has continued to be a constant source of support and guidance. In 1985, he and his partner, Stuart Brodsky, asked me to join their staff at Westside Veterinary Center, where I see feline patients and frequently work with hospitalized cats. I also administer therapy and guidance to the adoptees and adopters of Westside's Pet-I-Care, their program that places abandoned and rescued cats, dogs, rabbits, and birds. Drs. Brodsky and Cavanagh have supported my work, and it continues to be a fulfilling relationship.

The Animal Clinic of New York, owned by Dr. Marco Zancope, is another veterinary hospital where I am in residence. I first met Dr. Zancope at Washington Square Animal Hospital when he was an associate of Dr. Ann Lucas. When he bought the practice Dr. Zancope inherited me, and I'm happy to say I'm pleased.

My working relationship with Dr. Ann Lucas and her associate, Dr. Dianne De Lorenzo, continues to flourish. Ansonia Veterinary Center is another source of my referrals. I especially enjoy bicycling over with my case reports and meeting their newest resident cat. Animal General is another constant in my practice. Dr. Richard Fried and I had worked on cases together when he was at Westside Vet. When he moved to Animal General, I was happy that our relationship continued, and he introduced me to Dr. Paul Howell and the rest of the staff. It continues to be a valuable and productive association.

It's not unusual for me to receive veterinarians' referrals from nearby boroughs. I have had a long working relationship with Dr. Jay Luger's Cat Hospital in Queens, Dr. Michael Brodsky of Westchester County, and Dr. Marcia Landefeld of the Feline Veterinary Hospital in Nassau County. Many of my referrals are from across the country. I am on the board of the Humane Society of New York, where my book *Cats on the Couch* can be obtained, and all the proceeds go to the welfare of the adoptees. I have also worked with the A.S.P.C.A.'s departments of education and adoption and lectured at the Animal Medical Center in Manhattan on cat behavior. Dr. Cindy Bressler, formerly of Westside Veterinary Center, is one of the veterinarians there, so our working relationship continues much to my satisfaction, as Dr. Bressler is a credit to her field.

My house calls have included distant places, such as Kalamazoo, Michigan, and Hawaii, and my phone consultations have reached as far away as Australia, Alaska, Paris, and Naples.

I frequently speak at cat shows, such as the International Cat Show at Madison Square Garden in Manhattan, where I also answer questions at the *Cat Fancy* booth, which gives me the opportunity to meet many of my readers. Sheffield was one of my star patients at the Garden. But if he didn't stop abusing the judges, there was no way he was going to become a Supreme Grand Champion. After a couple of sessions and with the audiocassette that accompanied him in his show carrier, the judges couldn't believe this was the same cat. He collected his title and retired basking in his glory. He was a very contented Maine Coon.

I lectured at the veterinary school of Louisiana State

University. There, one of my co-workers was their feline mascot, and I used her to demonstrate my discovery that music therapy relaxes cats and helps to speed their recovery and increase their stress tolerance.

I am repeatedly asked, "What is a cat therapist? What is it that you do and how did you become one?" My answer is that I help people understand their cats' day-to-day needs, so that person and cat can relate in a way that promotes the emotional and physical health of both. But many of my cases involve cats who have already developed emotional problems that have precipitated behavioral disorders. Subsequently, emotional problems often trigger medical problems. That's why I feel it is imperative to treat the "total cat."

In the early seventies I first called myself a behaviorist, but people lumped me with B. F. Skinner, which didn't work. My methods are scientific and based on extensive observation, but I follow the intuitive method in which I regard the cat as a teacher and friend. I help make the cat's person aware of the needs and feelings of his cat—to get at the core of the problem—so the cat can be healed. The media referred to me as the "cat shrink." I realized I was doing family- or dual-species therapy. "Cat therapist" was the logical and appropriate label that evolved from my work with cats. My usage of "cat therapy" and "cat therapist" eventually caught on and has become part of the language.

In 1977 I was referred to as the country's founding mother of cat psychoanalysis and "Kitty Freud." My work was included in *National Geographic* in an issue devoted to wild and domestic cats. A photograph included a former patient of mine named Millie, whom I treated for timidity. She sat on a specially designed kitty chaise, and I sat nearby with pad in hand. The set was created to represent a Freudian dream. My biography was featured in *Biography* magazine in an article that related my story and included the work I did with two cats, Ben and Harry, to treat their grief and prepare them for a new home after the demise of their person. One of my many television appearances was in a segment for the PBS *Nature* series. It included a house call to cats Rafaella and Lippy, who suffered from office angst. Although they lived in the country, they also inhabited their person Elsie's office, and treatment was needed to quell their culture shock. I had worked with them on other issues, and Elsie explained how she felt confident that I would always be able to offer a practical and successful solution.

My international media coverage has included the London *Mail*, *Geo*, and several Japanese magazines. I've taped shows for London, German, Australian, and Japanese television. The Japanese appear to be great ailurophiles, and my book *Cat Talk* may be translated into Japanese, which would be quite an honor for me—to aid Japanese cats and their people. *Cat Talk* has already been translated into German and Danish.

People often ask me if I work with other animals, or do I only like cats. Horses are also a great love of mine. When I lived in Malibu I had a marvelous thoroughbred jumper named Capers. The late Capers taught me how to ride, and I strived to return my love when I groomed and bathed him. For several years I was a docent at the Central Park Wildlife Center, which greatly expanded my knowledge of animal behavior.

I'm very fond of dogs and selectively treat those with emotional problems. Dogs were the catalyst for my Montreal cat connection. When I was included in an article about dogs that was featured in *In Style* magazine, I received a call from Hot Dog Accessories in Montreal. When I mentioned that I had thoughts of occasionally seeing patients at the Ritz Carlton in Montreal (it's an animal-friendly hotel) and scheduling house calls in Canada, my idea was put into motion. I soon received a call from a journalist for the *Montreal Gazette*. I even did a session with Kiki, the journalist's cat, who was affected by the single-cat syndrome.

I did a session at the Ritz Carlton Hotel in Chicago with one of my former patients, who was once a very timid cat. Agrippina lived with her family in Chicago, and a tune-up session was needed because of a new baby in the family.

I derive much pleasure from teaching people to understand more about their cats. At one of my seminars for The Learning Annex, I met a gentleman named Philip Gonzalez. He had questions about one of his cats. When he mentioned that his dog Ginny had rescued a few of his cats, I knew that this was a story that had to be told. This became a reality, and Ginny's story is now told in not one, but two books.

Because my work involves other people's cats, I can always tell my cats' quips to my friends, Karen and Yvonne, who are cat-friendly but cat-less. Harriet is another such friend. In fact she was aboard when I started my telephone information service, "Pixie-All-About-Cats." Now and again she calls from Nantucket to tell me she caught my latest media piece. Frank, Esq., my long-time legal adviser, is, fortunately, a cat fancier. Harvey, my accountant, makes sure my cats are always provided for.

One of my former photographers, who went on to become an attorney, tragically took her life. Her three cats were left behind. I was able to console her family and guide the cats' sudden separation. One of my Christmas traditions was to have brunch with Nina and her family. Now without Nina, we take time to cherish her memory.

Because I do work with selected dogs, birds, and even goats, I also now call myself an animal companion therapist. Cats are my specialty, but I'm delighted to help other animals when I have the opportunity.

The two cats in my life now are Ziggy-Star-Dust and Diana-Moon-Dust. I adopted Star-Dust, a black cat, when he was a kitten in a Japanese restaurant, where he had lived briefly after he was found in the East Village. At the time, I needed a feral, cat-oriented kitten for my Siamese cat Sunny-Blue, a recovered attack cat, who needed a companion to dote on him exclusively—which Star-Dust did.

When Sunny passed on in August 1991, I lost not only a true friend but a co-worker. Because of Sunny's need for recognition, he had accompanied me on many of my television segments and when I did interspecies therapy at nursing homes or participated in other events. Because Sunny was Star-Dust's adopted papa and best friend, I expected Star-Dust would immediately need a Sunny look-alike, especially since Star-Dust was still very much feral. But I was in for a surprise. Star-Dust was suddenly quite interactive. He even chimed in with a meow when I recorded my announcement on my answering machine. However, he sounded like a Siamese cat because he had mastered Sunny's cry. He continued to sleep with me as usual and I decided I would await his cue before I adopted another cat. Five years passed by, and I continued to work with Star-Dust, who was no longer the phantom cat. But he was selective with my company. He now even permitted some visitors to stroke him as they admired his sleek, handsome looks.

When a female Siamese cat appeared with her male Siamese companion at Westside Vet, they were quickly adopted. Their original person had passed on and, before that, the female's former companion cat had also died. So she had had two major losses. Within a month after the two Siamese were adopted, the female was returned because she was sick with hepatic lipidosis, a disease of the liver. It's generally precipitated by stress, and causes a cat to become anorexic and the liver to become disabled. A chubby cat, such as this particular female, is usually a prime candidate for this disorder. Because of her triple loss she was also hit with separation anxiety. I worked with her to inspire her to fight for her life and regain the desire to be nurtured. She was given extensive medical care, including being fed via a stomach tube. The nurses and technicians gave her devoted attention and love. Finally, a few months later her stomach tube was removed and her starvation-level weight of five pounds started to very slowly inch upward. She was very needy and would throw herself into any available lap. I dubbed her Diana in honor of the Roman goddess Diana the huntress and protector of women. A cat is affected by the meaning and sound of a name, which is why I selected one of strength. I added "Lady" to elevate her role. Diana needed a home where she would be the only cat, as she always avoided Westside's resident cats, who had tried to win her over. But a few months passed and no such home appeared.

I decided to sponsor Diana and take her home, where I could continue to work with her. Star-Dust was now thirteen, and Diana was estimated to be eight. Because Star-Dust had lived with Sunny, another Siamese, he would be familiar with Diana's scent. He was still a cat's cat, and although Diana wouldn't be an only cat, she would benefit from his catsonality. Before I took her home, I had Star-Dust medically checked out to rule out any physical problems that might be precipitated by Diana's appearance. He was in top shape, so I brought her home and used my technique to introduce cats to each other. Lady Diana now was called Diana-Moon-Dust. It didn't take long for them to bond, and it is now Diana who grooms Star-Dust, but it is he who is intrigued by her presence.

Within the year Diana had developed inflammatory bowel disease, which is another result of her exceptionally stressful life. Like Sunny, Diana adores recognition, so she accompanies me on selected media appearances. Her acceptance of people is an inspiration for Star-Dust to increase his trust in humans. She's an ideal role model for him. Diana-Moon-Dust frequently joins me in my media appearances. She was a big hit on "Variety," the Children's

Charity telethon, and again on public television. Her contribution dramatically increased the pledges. Diana's a terrific media-mate because she loves the camera.

I don't have an associate yet, but there have been many who have contributed to my practice. Emily was the first. A reader of my *Cat Fancy* column, she wrote and asked if she could be my intern. This was a mutually rewarding experience, and Emily went on to graduate from Cornell Veterinary School. Morgan is a young, budding actress who worked for me as a coordinator. Jennifer, now an investment adviser, was another such person. I now work with Maria, a translator at the United Nations, who loves to visit the adoptees and hospital patients at Westside Vet. Serena is a high school student whom I met at the Animal Clinic of New York, my other hospital in residence. She did a yearly internship there as part of her school program, and I recruited her to assist me in various parts of my practice. Serena has become a surrogate me to my cats, and her invaluable presence continues as she enters her freshman year at New York University. Stacia, a pre-vet-student, is another former intern. She now works part-time in adoptions at the Humane Society of New York and consults me on various adoptees. She will be a very devoted veterinarian. Stacia was recently accepted at the University of Pennyslvania Veterinary School.

There are also those who are fascinated with my field and whose cats I've treated. My friend Ordway is such a person. More than a decade ago I introduced a new kitten, Rambo, to Bogie, his Tonkinese cat. When Bogie passed on a few years ago, Rambo was coupled with a kitten named Lucy, and the two are now a tight duo. I frequently receive cat-related press clips from Ordway or his wife, Jean.

For me to offer the best of myself to my patients and their caregivers, it is essential for me to be emotionally, physically, and spiritually healthy. My program includes cycle (spin), step, swim, and other classes at the New York

Health and Racquet Club, occasional races with the Gulf Coast Running Club, when I visit my sister Emily in Biloxi, and Jenny, a physical fitness trainer, comes to my apartment for workouts. Diana and Star-Dust usually participate. I'm also a volunteer at the New York Marathon. This has been an annual tradition of mine since the early '80s. I continue to take classes and attend meetings to extend my intellectual and spiritual knowledge.

I am a docent at The New-York Historical Society, which helps me to add other subjects to my information network so I'm not only "animal" literate. It may be that I'll help to put together an exhibit there on cats and other companion animals.

When people ask me what my favorite cat book is, my answer is *The Abandoned,* by Paul Gallico, which I read in the very early seventies. Its story is told from the point of view of a cat. Because it was a British version, the title was *Jenny,* the name of the cat from whose point of view the book was written. At The Cat Practice, this book was required reading for our new staff members. As I read this book I was able to truly understand something of how a cat felt and why a cat reacts as it does. In so many ways I realized that a cat's behavior is greatly influenced by emotions and instinct. This book was a marvelous spark to my understanding of how cats communicate. I recommend this book to anyone who wants a remarkable read, a piece of fiction that is so true to life.

When I decided to write *Cat Talk,* which concentrates on a cat's body language, I took classes at the Joffrey School of Ballet so I would be more in touch with my own body. A cat is a natural example of grace that a human has to make a supreme effort to master.

People ask me "What is it you do at your therapy sessions and how is it communicated to the cats?" My response is that when I conduct a session, I move, breathe, and talk in a manner that won't threaten the cat, who is instinctively so sensitive to these means of communication. The process consists of desensitization of the particular trauma. Because of my expertise and experience, the cat's caregiver feels calmer, and this is transferred to the cat, who begins to relax, and the associated trauma starts to defuse. The audiotape I make of the session, with New Age music in the background (because it's lowest in tension), is used to reinforce the therapy process. Finally, my specific recommendations on how to modify the cat's behavior are the sum of what can be called multidimensional therapy to a dual-special target.

I'm always adding new techniques. I use music therapy, a discovery of mine in 1984, because it is an alternative method that greatly speeds up a cat's recovery and increases a cat's tolerance of stress. I have a tape that instructs people and relaxes cats. Jesse, an amazing and courageous cat, was the conduit for this production. He was a cat who appeared at Westside Vet after he was rescued from a near hanging. After we had stabilized him medically and emotionally, he was adopted by a nearby boutique called The Cat Store. I settled him in with a session. Later, Yvonna, one of the proprietors, was responsible for the production and distribution of my "Cat Caring" tape, and Jesse's photo adorned the cassette box.

People have found the path to my practice in many extraordinary ways. A Long Island couple found me through their marriage counselor. At one of their sessions, they mentioned their only problem left was connected with their cat, Gucci. Their counselor referred them to a *Newsday* article that featured me, and they engaged me to help their cat.

Gerry Frank's book, *Where to Find It, Buy It, Eat It in New York*, was the catalyst for my treatment of an aggressive cat from New Jersey. His person turned to that book to find a restaurant in the theater district and came across my services as she turned the pages. Her mother sat in on the session, as she sometimes cat sat for Bo, and was able to apply some of my recommendations to her own cat.

I once flew to Washington as a birthday present from a young woman to her husband, who had mentioned that what he wanted most was a solution to their cat's indiscriminate defecation. When his wife read about me in *The New Yorker*'s "Talk of the Town," she contacted me, and the rest is history.

Battle Creek, Michigan, was another destination when a couple needed treatment for their cat Bart. They also wanted a program to relocate a group of outdoor feral cats they discovered when they moved to their new home. I'm truly happy when I can help feral cats.

Because of the patient and client intimacy that my practice involves, quite frequently the relationship turns to friendship after treatment has concluded. One such friendship is with two nuns, Mother Mary Joseph and Mother Teresa, who are at a cloistered monastery in New Jersey. Mother Mary Joseph first contacted me through *Cat Fancy* magazine and I did a phone consultation. The following year I made a series of house or monastery calls. We couldn't be in the same room because of their vows, but we could see one another, and the cats could roam at will. When one of their cats later passed on, I was able to connect them with a rescue group in Manhattan that had an adoptee who resembled their late cat. So Barnaby, a male cat rescued from the pound, went to live with Tookie and Silver Star—to defuse some of their female rivalry.

I've also attended weddings of many of my former clients. Courtney and Ned's cat, Monte, was the catalyst for my invitation to their wedding. Monte was severely timid and had low self-esteem and his feelings were expressed by indiscriminate defecation. So it was a victory for everyone—including his companion cat, Lola—when Monte gained in self-confidence and even graced their parties.

I also attended another wedding. I had successfully treated Jelly, the bride's cat, a now-reformed attack cat, before they married, and afterward did a session to integrate the couple's four cats.

I'm very pleased that I am sometimes engaged to work with several generations or successions of cats. In the early eighties I introduced a kitten named Jake to a young cat named Jamara. Several years later, after the demise of Jamara, I introduced another kitten, Chelsea, to Jake, and he quickly took him under his paternal paws with much affection. Their person, Joyce, is forever fascinated by their devotion. A couple in Connecticut have a cat, Mary, that I treated over ten years ago. Since then I have introduced a couple of new generations of cats, as the couple prefers to have four cats at all times. I even introduced their new puppy to this catdom, and she has taken on some very delightful feline characteristics. I feel honored when people rely on my expertise.

Cats have also reconnected me with old friends. Penny had read my column in *Cat Fancy*, and I was able to do a session with her cat Stoney, who had adopted Big Mike, a huge cat from her garden who defended Stoney against any alien cats. Sheril, another friend, saw one of my television segments, and I assisted her in the socialization of a cat family that moved in on her porch. It's always a thrill to see feral cats accept human friendship.

One evening I received a call from an old friend who needed my services to introduce a new cat to her female cat Max. I had introduced her former cats, and Marta wanted to keep the tradition alive. Loisina, another friend, gives her cat Sabrina an annual party, and a relaxation session from me is one of Sabrina's gifts.

I also treated Junior, a sweet male cat with severe anxiety, which he expressed by indiscriminate urination. His seven feline companions later succumbed to feline leukemia, but their person, Barbara, was able to prolong their lives way beyond the expected. She now has four females, who were all rescues, and they have slowly settled in. Recently, an endearing neutered male took up residence on

Barbara's patio, and I did a session to pave the way to his integration with the "gals."

My clients are always from all walks of life. A cat is not a social climber. Those in the health care profession are usually quite caring of their cat's health and psyche. I'm reminded of a cat named Foxy whose person, a psychologist, sought my counsel to tame Foxy's aggressive ways. Elisabeth is another psychologist whose cats I've worked with. Because my work involves two species, these women have become unofficial associates.

Those of the writing profession also frequently seek my services. Mambo is a cat I treated who outlived her younger companions. Her person is a writer for *The New York Times*. Mr. Gray, who was inherited from a friend, is a sports editor's cat with a bundle of problems. Fortunately, Mr. Gray's in the right hands. His person has a bundle of compassion and understanding. Mazel is a young cat rescued from the midst of traffic by a family who didn't intend to keep him with their other two older cats. I was able to provide them with the right introduction, and Mazel's now the top cat of a four-cat catdom. I'm called on to do a tune-up whenever there's a snag. My cat practice has been an influence on friends' cat acquisitions. My friend Mary Ann adopted Beau and Buster, who inspire her work. My editor Sarah also rescued a young kitten she named Vera.

"Your voice is heard so often on the cats' audio cassettes that you've become one of the family," Gregg, one of my old-time clients, frequently tells me. Ever since I worked with her late cat Cleo, I pop by to smooth out any current cat snags.

It's not unusual for me to receive referrals from cat communicators and spiritual healers. Two of these people are Gail De Sciose and Joanna Seere. I also receive requests for such alternative sources. Feline care-givers combine many therapeutic devices when their cats are in need.

Because I do extensive media, my brother-in-law, Ed Ouimette, a technophile, made a videocassette of my television clips, and I soon acquired my media agent, Paige Wheeler, a former associate of my literary agent. My brother-in-law, Tony Ganz, has referred care-givers in need from one coast to another. Yes, my sisters' spouses have certainly nurtured my cat practice—truly a family affair.

I frequently receive calls from rescue workers such as City Critters to help with emotionally troubled adoptees. One of my former interns works at The Humane Society of New York, and she will consult me about adoptees there that need special treatment.

I've always had an affinity for substance and old-world charm—such my inherent natural attraction to cats, appreciation of vintage cars, the Pierpont Morgan Library (where I was once a volunteer), and my old Smith Corona manual typewriter. When I began this book I considered buying a computer; however, the cat network stepped in. My friend Ellen and her husband own a computer-training school—whose resident cat is C.E.S.—and when I mentioned to Ellen my desire to learn the computer to speed up the production of my manuscript, Ellen thought this would be counterproductive, and she recommended that I put the computer literacy on hold until I finished my book. Ellen's cat Phoebe is a wonder. I always sensed something exquisite about Phoebe when I helped introduce two companion cats to her. Phoebe is now a senior cat and was recently diagnosed as being sightless. Phoebe clearly mastered her handicap. Lisa, a dear friend, whose cat, Max, I had treated for timidity, very generously offered to transfer my typewritten work to a disc. I've decided to upgrade to an electric typewriter before I make the big plunge into computers. Karin, a friend whose cats I treated for serious feuding, offered to lend me hers, since she's now computerized.

I can thank Piper, a saucy Siamese cat from Westport,

Connecticut, for my business brochure. Nearly two decades ago his person, Susan, had read my first book, *Cats Prefer It This Way,* and arranged for me to make a house call to treat a bit of new-cat competition between Piper and his two companions. Later, after Piper passed away, I introduced Skye to Nantucket. I particularly remember the day of this introduction because it was my birthday, and I had also participated in a broadcast for the BBC with a few distinguished celebrities such as Morley Safer. To me a working birthday is a terrific tribute. Anyway, Susan is a computer whiz and has always been the guiding force behind my brochure—for example, she reminds me when it should be updated. When she was a photojournalist she did many of my publicity photos, including the photo on my book *Cats on the Couch.*

Sasha is another cat whose person didn't discover he was blind until he was a few years old. His athletic demeanor and extroverted ways were certainly no giveaway. He was always a bit pushy with his companion cat, Chloe, which could be a result of his handicap. But like Phoebe's, his adaptation was remarkable. His person, Roberta, makes sure she doesn't move her furniture without walking Sasha slowly through the changes.

I constantly try to be flexible with my cat-related beliefs and principles. But the removal of a cat's claws has always been a "forbidden" with me. Ricky is a young cat who almost went under the knife but was saved at the last minute. He was a recovering feral cat that I had worked with who had been adopted as a companion for a cat who needed a cat-oriented cat. Several months later the person decided she had to have Ricky declawed. But the cat goddess was on guard. The person was unable to put Ricky into his carrier and decided that perhaps her decision wasn't right for him—so she would give him up instead. He was quickly adopted by a young couple, whose two cats Boo and Zucca took to Ricky at first sight.

When I signed this book contract in 1996, I never dreamed that four editors and three years later would be the drawn-out outcome of this creation. Fortunately, I received much support from my agent, Stephany, who persevered to clear any obstacles. My sister Gail reminded me that one of her films took nearly nine years to start production. Phyllis—my long-time friend and an editor, whose late cats Tulip and Barnaby cuddled up together on my very first manuscript when Phyllis took it home to read—never doubted that my book would reach fruition. Phyllis's current cats are Pansy and Sweet William, and they are the sweetest cats. Willy is a suave mover and shaker, and Pansy is more like a ballet dancer who chooses the right moment to communicate her every desire.

I have a long-time friend who was once an ailurophobe. She reluctantly accepted my invitation to temporarily share my apartment and also to cat sit for my then cats, Oliver and Sambo, while I was in California. Sambo's antics often frazzled Susan. But at bedtime he would join Oliver as he tucked into bed with Susan for the night. Now over two decades later Susan lives with her cats, Buddy and Elisabeth, and a dog named Charlie. When they're not out in her garden, the trio surrounds Susan on her sofa or wherever she hangs out. Susan often remarks how she is a recovered ailurophobe and, I might add, a fine ailurophile.

I once made a house call outside Philadelphia to a couple's cats, Rainbow and Lily, for stress reduction. When Rainbow later had to be hospitalized, the audiotape of her session accompanied her, and the staff played her the tape. When they didn't she would get their attention in a catlike fashion. Now many years later their daughter chose me as her role model at her school's career day assembly. What an honor for me!

Piffi and Mini were two cats I worked with in Los Angeles. Maria and Wolfgang, their people, flew me out a few times to treat their timidity. Wolfgang and Maria, their people, are in the film industry. Later, when Piffi was ill, they were working on a Clint Eastwood film. Eastwood was able to tell how Piffi was doing by Wolfgang's spirits. One day when Wolfgang was especially cheerful, Eastwood remarked how Piffi must have turned the corner, and she had!

Lois, another friend whose cat Casey I treated for the attack-cat syndrome, was always there with a suggestion when the editorial tide changed. I'm happy to say that Sarah, my present editor, has been worth waiting for. Aren't I lucky to have her signature! My illustrator is also an ardent cat lover, and his work reflects his feline appreciation.

My three siblings have certainly been in my court. My sister Emily and her husband have a dog Princess—no cat in their household—but they always have my books available for their many cat-caring friends. My brother, Bern, and his family frequently tell me that their cats, Buddy and Rainy, will benefit by yet another of my books. My sister Gail and her husband have a cat named Geli, and Gail has befriended Bugsy, a once feral cat who lives on the movie lot where Gail has her production company. Bugsy and Geli would never be a good match, so Gail provides for Bugsy's welfare on the movie lot. When Gail is away, she makes sure someone else takes over caring for Bugsy.

A friend once told me that cats are my religion. This was a compliment! I have never met a cat that I didn't like. I feel that I have helped to pave a new and nurturing path to cat mental health. One day I would like to have a training center where I can impart my knowledge to others who can carry on my work. A television spot or web site would also help me to address the many cat issues.

My goal is to continue to take a day at a time to strive to provide the best of myself for my patients and clients. They deserve no less!

Preparations for Life with a Cat

CHOOSING THE RIGHT CAT

The big moment has arrived. You've decided that a cat or kitten will brighten your life. What could be better than the company of such a companion? But should you get a cat or a kitten or one of each? What do you do? Why not visit a nearby shelter and see how the cats and kittens interact with you? Make several visits to form a realistic opinion of which you prefer.

If you're sure a cat is really for you, I congratulate you. The love of a cat or kitten will be a treasure. You've always admired the exquisite sensitivity and sensibility of cats. Now you're ready to reach out and choose a cat that's right for you.

Purebreds versus Domestic Cats

You may have heard that it's better to adopt a purebred cat because you can be sure of its disposition, whereas the disposition of an ordinary, mixed-breed cat is an unknown. That's partly true, but, although there are characteristic temperaments that are usually associated with a particular breed, there's no guarantee that the purebred cat you adopt will match your expectations. While most Siamese cats have a very distinctive meow, not all Siamese are alike. Similarly, most Persian cats are low key, but there are exceptions.

If you have your heart set on a particular coat color, coat length, and general temperament, though, your most likely option is the specific breed you've identified. You can also refer to books on cat breeds and perhaps visit breeders of the type of cat that interest you. But unless you're captivated by a particular breed, don't rule out a domestic short- or longhaired cat.

If you're not sure which to choose, do what a cat would do: take time before you make your decision. A cat washes when in doubt. You could take a cat nap for clarity.

Shelters

You may want to adopt a cat or kitten from a shelter. Most shelters are private nonprofit organizations and have their own bylaws. They are unlike city or state shelters that usually must accept any animal brought to them. Because of the large unwanted and stray population of domestic cats and dogs, the numbers of animals brought to these shelters are staggering and many don't make it out alive. Though a private shelter can be a no-kill facility, it is nearly impossible for a municipal shelter to adhere to such a policy.

Most shelters welcome volunteers to spend time with the adoptees. This may be an ideal way for you to choose a new cat or kitten and/or a fine way to increase your cat friends without a commitment.

Cats versus Kittens

If you're obsessed with neatness, must have everything in its place, and prefer a low-energy companion, a cat, rather than a kitten, would probably best suit you. A neutered cat who appears to be mellow and people-oriented would be a good match for you. Gender can be based on your preference, but remember each female and male has his or her individual catsonality. (I've coined the word "catsonality" to avoid the anthropomorphism inherent in "personality.") If you're not a neatness freak, you're not bothered by mischief and high energy, and you've never had a cat before and you want to help influence and develop its disposition, try two kittens, at least eight weeks old. They would be buddies for each other and won't be tempted to trash your belongings out of loneliness.

Single Cat versus Two Cats

If you spend a lot of time at home and prefer one cat, try to locate a cat that lived in a one-cat household and adores the role of "only" cat. Frequently, cats rescued from the street, who have had to battle other cats and harsh elements for survival, prefer to live without feline companions.

If you spend a lot of time away from home, you might want to consider two cats instead of one. It's not difficult to locate two cats that are buddies who need a home together.

You could even adopt two cats from different sources and separate them initially so they can view each other without physical contact. Chapter 8 explains how to introduce one cat to another.

Kitten or Adolescent Cat

You might consider adopting a kitten and a young adolescent, or even a kitten and an older cat, so the kitten will have an in-house tutor. This arrangement is also attractive economically, because you save on vaccinations and cost of spaying or neutering the adolescent or full-grown cat.

I consider an adolescent cat to be in between six to fifteen months old, a young cat from fifteen months to two years, and an adult cat from two years and up. But there's many an adult cat who has the look and spunk of an adolescent.

Child-oriented Cat

Suppose you and your husband have a six-year-old daughter and a four-year-old son who desperately want a kitten, but you're not sure that you can cope with another youngster. The ideal match would be a young cat that has formerly lived with children and is tolerant of and pleased by their attention.

But if it must be a kitten, don't adopt one that is less than eight weeks old so the kitten can retreat from your children when desired. A spunky kitten would welcome your children's playfulness. Opt for a shorthair so grooming isn't a major issue.

Cat for Senior Citizens

Your parents have always loved cats but haven't had one since their last cat passed on. They would like to adopt again and are perfect candidates for an adult cat that is at least six years old and prefers to be the only cat. If your parents are high-energy people, you can help them select a vivacious cat. Otherwise, you'd probably want to opt for a mellow lap cat.

A kitten would be appropriate only if your parents could take a part in the early upbringing and enjoy the antics and high-activity level of a kitten. I would try to persuade them to adopt an adolescent or young cat instead, if an adult cat is not their preference.

Whichever cat or kitten you decide on, be certain it has had a thorough physical examination. Also, have another potential home in mind for the cat in case your parents decide they don't want a cat after all.

Mistaken Ideas About Cats

You're under the impression a cat needs very little care, that it's fine to leave a cat alone weekends with lots of food and that it prefers to be alone—which suits your frantic schedule perfectly.

A cat is actually very dependent on its human for attention. An indoor cat is especially affected by its living situation, because it can't be resourceful in the way that an outdoor cat can. An outdoor cat can move on to another home if it feels neglected.

Don't adopt a cat believing that it's self-reliant. You could end up with a very unhappy and even sick cat.

Adaptability

If you're a city dweller, you may have wondered if it's fair to keep a cat indoors all the time.

Cats are very adaptable creatures. I've even known of country cats that have adjusted to living in a city apartment. If you provide them with stimulation and suitable companions, the transition is smooth. Adopt a young kitten or cat that is already accustomed to indoor living. There are some cats that appreciate a walk outdoors—on a leash, wearing a harness—but this is usually an acquired taste. Many cats that have been abandoned and rescued from the street have no desire to return—even briefly.

PREPARATIONS FOR THE ARRIVAL

You've made your decision and you're thrilled and excited. You'll need your cat to be comfortable when it arrives, and you'll also need to prevent any major and unnecessary catastrophes. Make preparations for this momentous occasion.

Supplies to purchase:

- Sturdy, well-ventilated cat carrier, lined with strips of newspaper (in case of calls of nature) to carry your new cat home; an identification tag can be purchased or created if not included with the carrier

- Cozy cat bed (but unless you're against your cat sharing your bed, you'll probably soon have a new bed mate)

- Litter box, scoop, and cat litter (I prefer a litter that's dust free, flushable, and biodegradable). A covered litter box may mask unpleasant odors, but an uncovered one is easier to scoop. A three-piece screen can be purchased or made to cut down the amount of scattered litter and provide a semblance of privacy. There's a plastic scooper with a handle shaped like a cat's face (this is made by Pet Buddies). It will add a touch of whimsy!

- Sturdy scratching post that won't topple over. An inferior one may cause him to turn to your furnishings for a pedicure and exercise. I recommend the Felix post and scratching board that are covered in sisal and scented with catnip. (Call Felix Company, in Seattle, WA, at 206-547-0042, or call Karate Kat at 800-822-6628. They are located in New York State and manufacture a similar post.) Most cats prefer to dig their claws into this type of fabric, so look for these qualities in a scratching post. If your cat also likes a wood surface, provide him with a block of wood that won't splinter. Many of the pet supply shops have wood cat trees (consult cat magazines, such as *Cats* and *Cat Fancy*, for inspiration, or you can build a cat tree if you're craftsy-inclined).

• Food and water dishes. These should not be plastic because plastic can contain chemicals that can sometimes cause a cat to develop acne on his chin or face. Also avoid pottery with a lead-based glaze, because it can be toxic. Once you have found good dishes, look for a tray or placemat to put under the dishes, to serve as your cat's table and protect your floor. You can have cat food on hand if you know the specific food preference. See Chapter 2 for more information on your cat's diet.

• Make or purchase a sticker for your house or apartment to alert rescue personnel that a cat resides inside, in case of fire or other emergency.

• A rubber cat brush or combs because you'll want to acquaint your new cat with daily grooming. Generally, a longhaired cat's fur is combed, and a shorthaired cat's fur is brushed. See Chapter 2 for more information on grooming.

Things to do:

• Cat-proof your home. Install window screens, remove toxic plants, store cleaning supplies and such things as pins, needles, tacks, and nails out of reach, and put away breakable ornaments. Most cats like to climb to high territory and also seek sanctuary under the bed or in a closet.

• Close the flue in the chimney if you have a fireplace. You don't want your new cat to end up in the apartment above or on the roof.

- Prevent domestic mischief with good housekeeping. Otherwise he may assume that uncovered garbage or dishes in the sink are playthings.

- Ward off your cat's destructive antics by distracting him with a toy, saying "no" sharply, or spritzing him with water from a plant mister. If you don't want your cat as a table centerpiece while you eat, remember to be consistent so your cat isn't confused by your indecisiveness.

- Load your camera with film so you can take some photos of your new cat. A special album will be filled in no time.

- Become acquainted with your neighbors who are cat lovers because you might need a cat sitter, and a friendly neighbor is ideal (be prepared to return the favor). There are even those cats who enjoy play dates, so get to know the neighboring cats.

- Think about who you could rely on to take care of your cat in case of an emergency—almost like a godparent—and with whom you could share your joy.

- Treat yourself to a subscription to *Cat Fancy* and *Cats* magazine to keep you in touch with current cat news.

- Select a name for your cat. The name may describe his behavior, the way he looks, or simply be one that reminds you of a person you knew or place you visited that you fancy. Such a name will fill you with happiness when you say it, and your cat will be included.

- Locate a reliable, competent veterinarian for your cat. Schedule an initial checkup. Your cat-loving friends can usually direct you to the best one. Prevent potential behavior problems with a behavioral consultation, especially if this is your first cat.

Arrival and Settling In

Today is the arrival. What should you do first? Remember that this is going to be fun, so relax! You're on your way to the start of a happy relationship.

When you arrive at your pet's current home, talk to your new cat or kitten softly, breathe freely, and think of all the fun you're going to have together. Your good feelings will be transferred to the cat because cats are sensitive to a person's tone of voice and posture, and are naturally empathetic. Soothe him with gentle words as he is placed in the carrier you've prepared for him, and keep talking to your cat during the journey home.

As soon as you arrive home, go into the bathroom and place his carrier beside the litter box, shut the bathroom door, and open the carrier. The newcomer will emerge at his own speed. You can introduce him to the litter box by gently lifting him into it.

After he familiarizes himself with the bathroom, open the door and allow him to explore one room at a time. This will prevent disorientation as he checks things out. Direct him to his bowls, scratching post, and any other key items.

Provide water but wait until he's comfortably acquainted with his new home before you feed him. You don't want your newcomer to suffer a stomach upset. Don't be surprised if he's not hungry at first. If his lack of appetite continues for more than a day, though, consult your veterinarian.

Don't plan any parties or housewarmings until your new cat settles in. A few visitors are okay, but don't overwhelm him.

If you prefer your bedroom to be off limits to your cat when you sleep, wish him a cheery good night with a hug and a kiss. Tell him you'll see him in the morning. Then make sure to close the bedroom door.

Although a cat is nocturnal, he can't see in complete darkness. If your home gets very dark at night, a night-light is recommended.

The first few times you leave your cat alone in the house, remember to say good-bye to him face-to-face. Not only does this make him feel loved, but it will ensure that he's not accidentally locked away in a closet or drawer. Tell him you'll see him later and think of him a lot. This is an especially important habit when your cat is new but it is not a bad habit to continue even after your cat has settled in.

If it's imperative that a repair person do work in your place before your cat has settled in, sequester your cat in another room with his food, litter box, and toys, or at least warn the person that you have a cat so he's not accidentally let out or terrified. Remind the person to keep unscreened windows closed.

Above all, take the time to get to know your cat. If you can arrange to spend the day at home when the cat first arrives, so much the better. You will cherish these memories.

Everyday Diet and Grooming

DIET

A cat's emotional and physical well-being is affected by diet. Yes, your cat *is* what he or she *eats.* Not only will a nutritious and well-balanced diet help your cat look and act her best, but a good diet is also one of the most important things you can give your cat in order to prevent medical problems.

Your cat's primary diet should consist of beef, beef by-products, or poultry, either cooked by you or purchased as canned cat food. Avoid canned cat food with ingredients listed as meat or meat byproducts; these can contain horsemeat, pork, or other ingredients that are troublesome for allergic cats. "Pure beef" on a label means the food contains beef or beef byproducts, but all the ingredients should be plainly listed on the label of canned cat food. If in doubt, contact the manufacturer.

Don't feed your cat raw meat because it can cause toxo-plasmosis (a cat disease that is also a major threat to pregnant women). Cooked or canned organ meats—such as kidney, heart, and liver—should be limited to less than one third of the weekly diet, as they are deficient in many essential nutrients.

Limit fish to a fourth or less of your cat's weekly diet. Avoid tuna, although many cats like it, because it can sometimes cause a vitamin E deficiency in cats and can trigger urinary, skin, and nervous/aggressive disorders. Feline tuna junkies are not uncommon. Your cat becomes addicted! Eliminate fish completely from your cat's diet if it becomes an obsession. You want to keep it from becoming an addiction, because then your cat may reject other food and won't receive the proper nutrition.

Limit dry and semimoist foods to one third of your cat's daily diet. There are those cats who thrive on a diet of the latter, but the majority of cats do better—health, coat, and catsonality-wise—on canned and/or people foods. In addition, a chronic predisposition to urinary problems can be provoked by dry food unless you feed a type prescribed by your cat's vet or formulated for cats with urinary problems. However, there is some controversy even to the use of such dry food.

Baby food is sometimes an acceptable supplement to your cat's diet, and there are cats who adore the meat, poultry, and vegetable varieties. Some cats even enjoy the fruit! Before you try those out, though, you should have your veterinarian check the ingredients to rule out any that might be harmful for cats.

Raw and cooked vegetables and fruit are fine for your cat, as long as they don't provoke digestive problems. A cat is a natural carnivore, though, and won't survive on a vegetarian diet.

Tasty dairy snacks, such as yogurt and cheese, are good foods for cats. Some cats are wild about milk, but it can cause diarrhea. Cream or half-and-half usually doesn't have this effect.

You can aid your cat in passing fur balls with a few pats of butter three times a week. If your cat dislikes butter, your vet can recommend a commercial gel, such as Petromalt or Laxatone.

It's not uncommon for cats to have unusual food passions. Melon, pitted olives, and asparagus are only a few. Spaghetti, pizza, ice cream, Twinkies, and blueberry muffins are others that shouldn't be overindulged because of their high caloric content. Use your judgment. You don't want to cultivate an insatiable passion in your cat for anything unhealthy.

Give your cat some good gum exercise with cooked chicken necks and backs. Other chicken parts can be dangerous to your cat. Cats sometimes also enjoy a rawhide dog toy.

Fresh water should always be available. If your cat makes a game out of tipping his water bowl, purchase a weighted one or put his bowl within a larger bowl so if it tips over, you don't have a flood. Many cats seek out the tub drain or drink water straight from the faucet. The earthy cat chooses to drink from the toilet bowl, but that can be hazardous if toilet bowl cleaners are in the water. There are now special water fountains for cats that you can fill with specially bottled or spring water.

There are vitamin supplements that you can purchase from the veterinarian or pet supply store. Brewer's yeast, in flake or powder form, and wheat germ are food additives that help make your cat's fur glossy. The yeast, which is high in B vitamins, also helps ease nervous stress. Brewer's yeast also comes in tablets, and there are those cats that gobble them up and come running when they hear the rattle of the container. But limit your cat's intake to two or three tablets daily. Stop using additives if they cause diarrhea or stomach upset. Brewer's yeast should not be given to a cat with a known bladder or urinary problem. Mix additives well in your cat's food so the taste is not as strong.

Feedings

It's generally best to feed your adult cat twice a day with a snack or two in between. Feed a kitten four times a day until he is five months old, with three daily feedings until he is six months old. (See Chapter 4 for more information on kitten care.) Wash and refill the water bowl at least twice a day. Nine ounces or more of food should be sufficient for a kitten's daily intake. For young cats, six months to a year old, seven or eight ounces daily should be adequate. Provide five or six ounces of food a day for a cat over a year old. Your cat's size and weight should also be your guide to quantity.

Protein and fat should be the primary ingredients in your cat's diet. However, senior cats need a different diet. (See Chapter 16 for more information on senior cats.) There are cats who cannot digest carbohydrates easily. Sometimes a cat instinctively will eat what's best for him and avoid what upsets his system, but usually your guidance is needed.

If you have more than one cat, there can be a communal bowl for water and dry food snacks, but each cat should have an individual dish or bowl. A place mat or tray beneath the dishes helps keep the floor clean if your cat is a messy eater. For example, there are cats that like to scoop food up with their paw, and some like to transfer food from their plate to the floor. If your cat is a hasty eater, who almost inhales his food like a vacuum cleaner and tends to vomit immediately afterward, you'll appreciate having his dish on a place mat.

Routinely wash out your cat's plates after each feeding.

Cat-friendly Greens

An outdoor cat relies on natural greens to aid his digestion. Eating grass enables a cat to vomit and calm an upset stomach. Many an indoor cat enjoys greens for the same reasons. But not all greens are cat friendly. There's a long list of houseplants that are objectionable and some that are even lethal to cats. You can phone the National Animal Poison Control Center, but there is a fee for their advice (800-548-2423). Most veterinary hospitals have a list of the hazardous or poisonous plants.

If you prefer that your cat not nibble your houseplants, hang them in unattainable spots or position them totally out of reach.

Not all cats are plant eaters. But if your cat is, you can plant a pot of grass for leisurely nibbles, so your cat will have his own grass and not have to seek out your plants. Plant two or three so your cat's supply is endless. Containers of grass for cats can be purchased from health food or pet supply stores. Praise your cat as he nibbles.

Asparagus or celery sprouts provide a tasty graze for some cats and are available in small pots at many large markets or gourmet shops.

It's a good idea to place a mat under your cat's greens so any scattered dirt or grass is easy to clean up.

Weight Problems

PUDGETTE

It's not uncommon for cats to selectively eat food containing nutrients they may be deficient in. This instinctive act sometimes alerts their people to the particular deficiency. But, like people, cats can also eat more than is good for them. However, weight gain can also be a sign of illness. If you suspect you have a pudgette, rule out any medical problems for the weight gain with a complete physical exam. Once your vet has determined that your cat is healthy, you'll need to start changing your pet's eating patterns. A bit of extra flesh can be cute or a lifesaver in an emergency. Some cats are born to be big. But if your neutered male resembles a pregnant female or your spayed female resembles a blimp, you have a genuine pudgette. You don't want your cat's excess weight to stress the heart or cause other physical problems. The following tips will turn the fat tide.

How to slim down Pudgette:

- Curtail your cat's snacking habits and make sure his daily feedings aren't overgenerous.
- Divide four and a half ounces of food into three feedings a day if your cat's acceptable weight is in the range of nine to eleven pounds. The extra feeding should persuade Pudgette he's eating more.
- Feed Pudgette some melon or vegetables that are low in calories if he pesters you for more food. But remember, calories do add up, so don't overdo!
- Take Pudgette for a walk in the hall or toss a few favorite toys for him to chase—a cat in motion burns more energy than a resting cat. Remember to be enthusiastic, and mean it. A game before feeding should create a pleasant association, such as that food is preceded by fun.
- Play with animal friends will also help. Perhaps you can arrange play dates with a neighbor's dog if Pudgette is the only cat around.
- Adopt a feline friend for Pudgette to step up his metabolism. If Pudgette inhales all of your second cat's food, feed the new cat separately. If he needs company, stay with him. There may be a food that Pudgette abhors that you can feed the new cat.

- Try one of the special prescription foods for over-weight cats that are available from the veterinarian or try a commercial cat food formulated to be low in calories. Be sure not to triple up the low-calorie portions and defeat the purpose.

Your cat's appetite might have ballooned out of frustration. Did you feed him every time he cried or ran to the food dish? If so, you unwittingly contributed to a food obsession. The next time this happens, distract your cat with a game or toy. It may be your cat merely needs more contact. Affection is a terrific substitute for food. But it may take a while to change his routine. Remember, this obsession didn't appear overnight. You must be constant and sincere in your efforts. Your cat is what he or she eats, and you're in control of the food. Love your cat with affection—not food!

TWIG

If your spayed female or neutered male looks like a twig in spite of a very healthy appetite, take your cat to the vet. Parasites or other health problems can cause weight loss.

If Twig is in top shape but merely needs more food or is a picky eater, try the following tips to nurture Twig's lean body.

How to plump up Twig:

- Cook him chicken for the personal touch.
- Feed him by hand for that special royal treatment.
- Feed Twig several small meals a day. If you have several other cats of normal weight and they want more food, too, feed them more often but don't increase their overall daily intake.
- Make sure Twig's food is not being nibbled by one of your other cats. Distract your other cat if he tries to eat Twig's food.

- Ask your veterinarian whether high-calorie vitamin supplements or an appetite stimulant would be helpful.
- Get a second cat. A companion for Twig may be the inspiration to stimulate his appetite.
- Give Twig more attention. If your time is scarce, arrange for a neighbor, child, or professional cat visitor to be the surrogate you.

Your cat will live a happier and healthier life with the right input. What's more, you'll reap the dividends!

GROOMING

The rough surface of your cat's tongue makes it a perfect tool to wash his fur. This action massages the skin, stimulating circulation, bringing more oxygen to the skin and enhancing the coat. A cat feels warm and relaxed when he washes, and it reminds him of kittenhood and being lovingly washed by his mother cat's tongue. This is why your cat may suddenly begin to wash himself when he feels tense or in doubt. It's a marvelous feel-better habit.

A cat's coat frequently mirrors his emotional and/or physical well-being. Grooming is instinctive with a cat, but when a cat's energy level is low, the desire to groom often diminishes. This is especially true of a street cat, who can experience endless street dirt and is constantly on the run. Sometimes a cat's coat becomes so tangled that he must be anesthetized and shaved by a veterinarian. Don't let this happen to your cat. Daily grooming should be incorporated into your schedule, even if it's just a quickie.

Longhaired Cats

It's usually preferable to use combs of various widths on a longhaired cat. Grooming should be a daily ritual.

To groom a longhaired cat whose fur is severely matted, gently cut out the large mats using a scissors with blunted tips. Keep one blade next to the skin, while you carefully cut up through the hair to slowly remove the mat.

Now you're ready to comb or brush. Be careful and gentle as you move over his body. Start with the favorite spots around the head and under the chin. Don't approach the rest of the coat until you have removed all the tangles there. The key is to be gentle but firm and not to pull on the skin. The more relaxed you are, the easier the grooming will be for your cat.

If combing your cat is not your cup of tea or your cat's, you might want to engage a professional groomer to come to your home. House calls are generally less stressful for a cat because your cat won't have to leave home and encounter unfamiliar scents and/or other animals.

Shorthaired Cats

Use a rubber brush. Dampen it to minimize the scattering of loose fur. Use a comb if the fur is very tangled.

If your cat doesn't like being brushed, try sitting on the floor while you groom him. Both of you will be more relaxed. Tell your cat what a terrific cat he is. Groom a little each day to increase your cat's tolerance. Approach him when he's sleepy so he'll be more receptive.

General Grooming Tips

End the grooming session by lavishing love and compliments on your cat to establish a positive connection between grooming and affection.

An egg yolk twice a week, a pat of butter once daily, or one quarter teaspoon of brewer's yeast daily in each meal will help stimulate healthier fur. Don't give your cat raw egg whites. Cook the egg whites if your cat craves them. Special sprays (such as Lo Shed) and vitamin supplements (such as Gold Caps) are available to enhance your cat's coat.

Your cat's physical appearance mirrors his inner feelings. Don't disregard what your cat's appearance tells you.

When grooming is a problem:

- Undergrooming—A physical problem can cause a cat to neglect his grooming. When a cat's fur is bedraggled, he usually feels awful, making him less active. Ungroomed fur can lead to skin infections that can cause him pain whenever he moves. Such pain can also precipitate urinary and respiratory problems.

- Overgrooming—Physical or emotional problems can cause a cat to lick persistently at one area, such as the stomach or leg. The site may become bald and inflamed. Take your cat to your veterinarian to check for a physical cause, such as a skin condition or an allergy. Often the veterinarian will give your cat an anti-inflammatory injection to ease the itching and discomfort. If your cat is overgrooming because he is anxious, he may need professional advice to discover the cause of the anxiety and suggest solutions, such as your spending more quality time with your cat, getting a second cat if your cat is lonely, or improving intercat relations if you already have at least two cats.

Bathing

Usually a cat's fastidious grooming precludes bathing, but if your cat does need a bath and you prefer to do the honors, select a time when you're most relaxed. It's a good idea to ask a friend to assist you. Remember: be calm and confident, gentle but firm. If your cat tends to be nervous, you might want to ask your vet for a tranquilizer. Do test it beforehand to make sure it will be effective. Sometimes the over-the-counter products sold in pet supply stores are effective.

Essential materials:

- tub or large sink
- sufficient lighting
- soft music that calms the senses of most cats and people
- cat shampoo or baby shampoo
- cream rinse or conditioner (a gentle human cream will suffice)
- Q-Tips
- hair dryer
- several large towels
- brush and metal combs
- scissors for clipping large tangles
- garbage bag for any extraneous fur, etc.
- mercuric oxide ointment to protect the eyes
- large pitcher or basin full of water for rinsing
- brown wrapping paper or plastic to spread on floor around sink or tub to absorb any water
- nylon net bag made especially for holding cats for bathing

A ribbon is optional and you may want to have a camera on hand to photograph the finished product.

SUGGESTED BATHING PROCEDURE

1. Start and continue to stroke and praise your cat during the bath.
2. Begin with the ears. Moisten the Q-Tips with luke-warm water and swab out just the visible part of

the inside of your cat's ears. You may need to gently fold the tip of the ear back. Do *not* try to clean
your cat's ear canal.

3. Gently apply a thin layer of the mercuric oxide ointment around the eye area to protect your cat's eyes
from soap.

4. Comb and brush your cat before you apply water
to the fur. A longhaired cat should be combed to
remove any mats. Start with the stomach area and
underparts. Separate any large tangle into smaller
ones. Don't try to attack the mat as a huge mass.
Talk soothingly to your cat as you comb him. Remember to work from the outer tip of the tangle in
toward the skin. Your cat is ready for the bath
when the comb goes freely through his fur.

5. Make sure the room temperature is warm. Close all
windows in the room where you are going to bathe
your cat so your wet cat won't get chilled. Close
the door to the room.

6. Hold your cat firmly but gently by the scruff of the
neck as you place him in the sink or tub. Wear
rubber gloves to protect your hands and a long-
sleeved shirt.

7. Slowly fill the sink or tub with about 4 inches of
warm water. Wet your cat's back, legs, and belly
thoroughly. You might want to add some rubber or
plastic cat toys to the water as a diversion.

8. Apply cat shampoo. Follow package instructions for
the amount. Work shampoo into your cat's fur.
Don't use too much shampoo, or rinsing will be
endless. A sponge to wet your cat's fur is optional.

9. Rinse him thoroughly with warm water. Use a
pitcher or the spray attachment on your sink.

10. Apply the cream rinse or conditioner. Rinse thoroughly again so your cat doesn't have a reaction to leftover shampoo or conditioner.

11. Wrap your cat in large towel and kiss and hug him.

12. If your cat will tolerate it, use the hair dryer but set the temperature to low. Fluff fur with comb or brush as you dry. If your cat is terrified of hair dryers, towel dry him and place him in a warm spot, such as a sunny windowsill or under a lamp.

13. If your cat becomes chilled, wrap him in a warm, dry towel or blanket. Hug him and your body heat will warm his body.

14. Give one final comb or brush and praise your cat.

15. Adorn your beautifully clean cat with a ribbon around his neck. Your cat can treat the bow as he chooses.

If this has been a stressful ordeal for the two of you, you might want to engage a professional groomer for the next bath. It's usually best to have your cat bathed at home where he'll be more comfortable in his own environment, rather than take him to the groomer's.

Not all cats need to be carefully coaxed into allowing themselves to be bathed! There are some cats who have a passion for water and will even join their person in the shower. Such a cat might welcome a needed bath.

MEDICAL PROBLEMS

Allergies

Sometimes a cat may be allergic to a particular food, cat litter, household cleaning agent, fabric, plant, fragrance, dust, tobacco, or medication—to mention the most common sources. The allergic reaction may be manifested by sores or inflamed skin, bald spots, vomiting, incessant coughing or sneezing, irregular bowel movements or urination, and runny eyes or nose. If your cat exhibits such symptoms, consult your cat's vet.

Frequently, extensive diagnostic work must be done to help identify the source of the allergen. It's not unusual for your vet to use the process of elimination and/or controlled exposure of your cat to suspected allergens to help make the diagnosis. Once the cause of the allergic reaction has been determined, treatments can include anti-inflammatory medication and/or a change of diet. Alternative medical techniques, such as homeopathic treatment or acupuncture, when combined with classical veterinary medicine, can also be effective in treating allergies.

Generally speaking, veterinary medicine has come a long way in the treatment of allergies, so the prognosis for an allergic cat is quite good. Because emotional stress factors into a cat's physical discomfort, a behavioral session with a therapist is recommended to reduce the stress and increase your cat's comfort and speed his recovery. (Consult your phone directory or veterinary hospital for names of a therapist.)

Your cat suddenly isn't himself. His behavior is highly unusual. You think he may be acting out of character because he's mad at you or feeling frustrated or deprived. If his behavior change is solved with an increase in attention, care, or diet, there's no need for further intervention. If these measures don't work, though, before you absolutely determine it's a behavioral problem, rule out any medical causes for your cat's bizarre behavior. A sudden change in catsonality or daily habits may be a symptom of a physical problem.

Other Medical Problems

The following catsonality changes are *symptoms* of your cat's discomfort and/or problem:

Ambivalence. Your cat appears to be ambivalent about your affection. Up until now, your cat was a lovebug. His ambivalence may be caused by physical discomfort, such as arthritis or a cardiac-related illness, or because of a particular nutrient or vitamin deficiency.

Demanding behavior. Your cat won't let you out of his sight. You usually don't object to his demands for attention, but his behavior seems a bit extreme. Your cat's constant need for attention could be a symptom of general physical discomfort that medication could remedy.

Aggression. Your cat was always a little saucy, but now he's become aggressive. Aggressive behavior can be caused by a physical problem.

Hostility toward your dog. Your cat has always adored your dog, but you've noticed that lately he's been grouchy with him. Your cat's sudden irritation with your dog may be because he is physically uncomfortable or ill. Such unusual behavior could also indicate that your dog has a medical problem. Your cat is sensitive to your dog's discomfort, which consequently makes him anxious, irritable, or elusive. He becomes aggressive toward your dog out of anxiety. The dog becomes his tension target.

Litter box misbehavior. Pristine litter habits were always the rule with your cat. Now you frequently find puddles or deposits outside the litter box or in and about your home. Untidy litter habits may be a symptom of diabetes, inflammatory bowel disease, constipation, asthma, a cardiac problem, kidney degeneration, a specific bladder problem, parasites, feline immune disorders, and thyroid abnormalities.

Excessive grooming. Your cat has recently begun to groom one spot incessantly until it's inflamed. Your cat's obsessive grooming may be an allergic reaction or caused by a vitamin deficiency, fleas, or other external parasites.

Crying for food. Food has become an obsession with your cat. He frequently cries for food, often into the wee hours of the night. But sometimes food doesn't pacify the cries.

And in spite of his food consumption, he remains thin. A thyroid disorder, anemia, a cardiac problem, or an enzyme deficiency could be to blame for your cat's food mania and slenderness.

Finicky eating. Your cat used to be a hearty eater, but now picks at his food. Lack of appetite may result from a dental problem, a digestive disorder, or a respiratory illness.

Vomiting. Your cat has vomited on your kitchen floor once or twice a week. It appears to be undigested food. Bouts of vomiting may be a result of a gastrointestinal problem, decayed or abscessed teeth, a food allergy, hepatic lipidosis, or pancreatitis.

Your cat's deviant behavior may also be a problem that is a combined emotional and physical problem. It's important to treat the total cat. The above outlined medical disorders are only potential causes to give you an indication of your cat's possible source of discomfort. They are also to alert you that the original source or stress target may not be causing the apparent symptom that you've noticed. Consequently, both the primary and secondary stress targets will have to be treated to remedy the problem. Your cat's health is dependent on your knowledgeable and nurturing care. Don't ignore your cat's signs of distress when you are the source of his eventual relief.

HOUSEHOLD DANGERS

High-rise Syndrome

It never occurred to you that a cat could fall from a window and become severely injured. What self-respecting cat would fall, and even if he did—he'd land on his feet!

Cats do not have good depth perception, so it's not uncommon for a cat to make a dash at a passing bird or object and take a disastrous topple. There is a theory that if a cat falls from below the fifth floor or from above the twentieth, he may escape injury. But why gamble with your cat's life? Terraces should be cat-proofed, or else *closely* supervise your cat when you let him out on the terrace. Windows should have full screens, or half screens should be inserted in the window so that a cat's paw can't push one aside.

Harmful Household Objects

You always thought a cat was savvy enough not to ingest what might be harmful to his health. Wrong! Protect your cat from his natural curiosity! The following objects can be fatal.

Antifreeze. The main ingredient in most antifreeze (although some cat-friendly ones now exist) is ethylene glycol. Its very sweet taste and smell attracts animals, but one lick can be deadly. Wood alcohol is an ingredient of other antifreezes that can also be fatal. Keep antifreeze out of your cat's reach. Cap containers securely and wipe up any spills.

Brooms. Ingested broom straws can result in possible throat, stomach, or intestinal perforation. Keep brooms out of reach.

Cleaning fluids, rodent and bug killers. The offensive scent of chemicals does not always prevent your cat from taking an experimental lick. But this one lick could be fatal. Chemicals, paints, poisons, cleaning fluids, garden supplies, and any other questionable substances should be kept out of reach and tightly capped. Powdered bug killer can coat your cat's paws if he walks through it. An attempt to clean his paws could prove fatal. Any edible insect- or rodent-killing products should also be avoided. Finally, cat toys can be a source of poison to your cat if they are affected by insecticide. A reliable professional exterminator can solve your problem of bugs or rodents with cat-friendly means. But you must do your part by removing all objects that can be a source of danger to your cat until the process is finished. Also beware of products that claim they are cat-friendly. Any object that a cat can lick, ingest, or inhale should be removed. (Consult your cat's veterinarian for any clarification.)

Dangerous toys. Beware of cat toys with loose bells or glued-on eyes or noses that could become loose, allowing your cat to swallow them. Keep your cat away from any small objects that he could ingest.

Garbage cans. Garbage containers should have a secure cat-proof lid, so your cat can't gain access. Wastepaper baskets can be overturned, so make sure that their contents are cat-friendly.

Household appliances. Cover any unused electrical outlets, and don't let your cat chew on electrical cords. Keep your cat away from any electrical appliance that's in use. Check the inside of a washing machine or dryer before each use to make sure your cat isn't inside. A refrigerator and oven are other places that your cat could curl up in.

Medicines. Consult your cat's veterinarian if your cat is sick and needs medication. *Don't assume* that what's good for your ailment is good for his! A mistake could be deadly. All medicines should be kept in tightly closed containers and out of your cat's reach.

Poisonous plants. There are plants that are especially deadly. Consult your cat's veterinarian, your librarian, the poison control center, or *Cat Fancy* magazine for a complete listing of poisonous plants.

Rubber bands and paper clips. These can be easily swallowed, so they should be kept in a drawer or container where they are out of reach of those curious paws.

Sewing supplies. Needles, pins, and thread should be put away after each use. Your cat may be very attracted to a threaded needle. Keep it out of his clutches. Finally, don't give your cat empty wooden thread spools to play with because they may splinter in your cat's mouth.

Sharp objects. Scissors, knives, safety pins, razor blades, and other such objects should be kept out of reach. Don't leave knives or forks in the dish drain where your cat can jump on them and receive a puncture wound.

Shopping bag handles. Cat-proof empty shopping bags by removing their handles. Otherwise, your cat may crawl in and catch his head in the handles.

String, yarn, dental floss, and drapery cords. Be sure you supervise your cat when he plays with string, yarn, or dental floss. Intestinal blockage, strangulation, or even death can occur if he swallows any of these. Used dental floss should be disposed of in a cat-proof waste can. Make sure there aren't any cords dangling from window shades, drapes, or blinds that your cat can become tangled in and injured.

Aluminum foil, corks, and cellophane. Your cat can be seriously injured if any of these articles are chewed or partially eaten and become lodged in his throat or stomach.

Claws and Exercise

CLAWS

A cat is born with claws because he needs them for defense, catching prey, balance, and grasp. Although claws can cause damage to objects or people, the removal of a cat's claws is unnatural, and the procedure is not without the potential for complications.

Removal of Claws

It's been a long time since you've lived with a cat. You adored your last cat, but your carpets and sofa were totally trashed. Your friend wants to give you two kittens for your birthday and you wonder if you should have them declawed. You know people who have had their cat's front claws removed, and your neighbor had her cat totally declawed.

In the early seventies, I co-wrote an article on why you shouldn't declaw a cat you love. My opinion remains the same twenty years later. Such an operation can trigger both physical and emotional problems, such as psychogenic dermatitis, bladder difficulties, aggressiveness, and severe timidity. There are many viable alternatives to declawing.

MODIFIED DECLAW

There is a new technique called tendonectomy where the tendons that flex the digits are severed so the claws can't be extended but will still continue to grow. There may be medical complications such as dermatitis on the nail bed. And how frustrating for a cat to have useless claws.

STANDARD DECLAW

A cat's balance, grasp, ability to catch prey, and ability to defend himself are greatly affected by the presence of his claws. All these are handicapped by the removal of a cat's claws, and the surgery is quite dramatic. The cat is given a general anesthetic. A guillotine nail cutter amputates the claw of each of the toes, resulting in ablation of the third joint of each toe. Bandages on the toes prevent hemorrhaging. These bandages are usually removed two to three days after surgery.

Complications

Potential immediate physical complications:

1. Adverse reaction to the general anesthetic can range from respiratory difficulties to death.
2. Gangrene—Tight bandages may cause the foot to become gangrenous, which can ultimately require amputation of the leg.
3. Hemorrhage—Many cats will begin to hemorrhage when the bandages are removed. New bandages will

have to be applied. Medication and additional hospitalization may be required.

4. Limping—Your cat may start to limp from discomfort.

Potential immediate emotional complications:

1. Temporary insecurity or aggression—Your healthy cat recovers from the anesthetic with throbbing and bandaged feet. He's confused and unhappy. This might cause him to become reclusive or aggressive.

2. Anxiety—He's frustrated by the bandages because they make it hard for him to stand and walk. Sudden bleeding makes him more anxious.

3. After the bandage removal, he discovers his claws are missing and it hurts when he walks. What happened to his graceful stride? He may even limp for a while, which frustrates him. His confusion increases, and he feels disoriented and insecure.

Potential later physical complications:

1. Regrown claws—If done incorrectly, this procedure can result in the incomplete removal of the nail bed of some or all of the toes. When this occurs, the result can be the regrowth of abnormal claws that are usually misshapen and useless.

2. Infection—If the trimmer was dull or your cat's bones were brittle, the bone could shatter. If a bone fragment is left behind in the paw, it can serve as a focus for infection. A follow-up surgical procedure under general anesthetic is the only remedy.

3. Other seemingly unrelated illnesses—Many chronic physical ailments, such as cystitis, asthma, and skin disorders, can be traced to the period immediately following declawing.

Potential later emotional complications:

1. Insecurity or aggression—The anxiety from the trauma of the surgery and postoperative confusion may affect him emotionally. Without his claws, he may become insecure and distrustful and begin to overcompensate for his lack of claws—his natural line of defense. Aggressiveness may result from his insecurity. When he's confronted by a new or threatening situation, he may overcompensate for his insecurity and be more apt to react by biting. A bite is more severe than a scratch.

2. Timidity—There are also cats that become reclusive and timid without claws.

MISCONCEPTIONS ABOUT CLAWS AND DECLAWING

Fiction: If your present cat is declawed, any subsequent cats you adopt must also be declawed.

Fact: It's not necessary to declaw a new cat because your present cat is declawed. Generally, a cat keeps his claws in when wrestling with a companion cat. A declawed cat can defend himself with hind claws or teeth.

Fiction: A cat has excellent balance and always lands on his feet with or without claws.

Fact: High-rise syndrome is common at veterinary hospitals. To land on his feet, a cat must flip over before hitting the ground. A fall from above the fifth floor is not usually without injury. Even if the cat does land on his feet, the force of the landing can still cause severe injuries. When a cat is declawed, his inherent grace and balance is affected, and he becomes even more vulnerable to a spill from a window ledge.

Fiction: Only an outdoor cat needs his front claws for defense.

Fact: Whether or not your cat goes outdoors, he still needs his claws for balance and presence of mind and body.

Fiction: Neutering and spaying is a surgical procedure for the welfare of a cat. Declawing is also a surgical procedure, so it must be for the welfare of the cat.

Fact: These two kinds of operations cannot be lumped together. A cat's *physical* and *emotional* health is not impaired when he or she is neutered or spayed. The surgery contributes to a better state of health for a cat who is in an environment where he or she can't procreate. On the other hand, a cat needs and uses his claws every day.

Fiction: When a cat has to have a leg or tail amputated because of an accident or illness, he usually recovers without any psychological problems. The same should apply to a cat who's declawed.

Fact: A cat who's had a leg or tail amputated has usually experienced pain in that particular part of his body. The source of anxiety is gone once the leg or tail is removed, and he can quickly adapt to the new situation. However, before a cat is declawed, his paws are not a source of pain. There is no negative association. Before the surgery, his paws felt fine. But when he awakens from the anesthesia, he experiences confusion and agony.

Although there are declawed cats who do not appear to have suffered any physical or emotional consequences, why take a chance with your cat's physical and emotional well-being? Many of the declawed cats that I have encountered in my cat practice have a lower tolerance of stress and are usually less self-assured.

Alternatives to Declawing

PURCHASE A GOOD SCRATCHING POST

Your cat's post should be one that won't let him down. It should be covered with a tough, scratchy material, such as a woven sisal, that your cat will love to dig his nails into. The post should be tall and sturdy so it will not topple over.

A sisal post, scented with catnip, that has a sturdy, balanced base can be ordered from Felix (3623 Fremont Avenue North, Seattle, Washington 98103, 206-547-0042). They also have a scratch board that especially pleases senior cats. You might be able to purchase these items at your local supply store. A similar post and scratch board can be ordered from Karate Kat at 800-822-6628 or 914-592-7233.

Many cats enjoy using a rectangular, two-foot-long corrugated cardboard scratching post, seasoned with catnip. It is sold at most pet supply stores.

Another type of post has a wooden foundation wrapped with twine. Some are shaped like a pyramid.

There are also large and floor-to-ceiling posts made of wood and covered with carpet called cat condos. They often have cubicles for a cat to hide in or platforms for cats to perch on. There are even floor-to-ceiling posts that are very similar to real trees for those cats that prefer wood to dig their claws into. Some are made from tree bark and also include carpet.

Unless you have a tiny place, you should give your cat an assortment of scratching posts. Sometimes it may take a few months for a cat to adapt to a new addition. You can donate the ones he rejects to a friend's cat or to a local animal shelter. But don't hesitate to purchase more of the ones he favors.

There are simple alternatives available for you and your cat. They can be purchased or made with your creative and handy resources. Your local lumber yard or hardware store can help you with the choice of materials.

INTRODUCING YOUR CAT TO THE NEW POST

1. Rub fresh catnip all over the post.
2. If your cat chooses to avoid the post, don't drag him over to it. Lure him by twirling the toy at the top of the post or slowly scratching the post with your fingers. If your cat doesn't respond right away, he'll go to the post when he's ready.
3. Place the post in an accessible spot or your cat may avoid it.
4. If your cat seems wary of the post, make it the center of his activities. Place the post next to one of his favorite hangouts.
5. Be sure to praise and stroke your cat whenever he uses his post.
6. When he tires of the toy at the top of the post, replace it with a new one.

How to Protect Your Furniture

Cover the furnishings that your cat may wants to scratch with an attractive blanket, afghan, or spread so your cat is not distracted by his old scratch targets. It might take at least a month for him to form new habits. Plastic shields can be purchased or made for the corners of a chair or sofa. A product called Sticky Paws can be purchased from a pet supply store. It consists of easily removable transparent adhesive strips you apply directly to the fabric. Such a surface will repel your cat.

A drop of Tabasco sauce on whatever soft furniture you want to protect sometimes is a great deterrent.

Distract your cat with a toy or game when he begins

to scratch your furniture. If he still doesn't obey, try a spritz of water from a plant mister. When you reprimand him, use a firm NO! When he stops, praise him.

Your cat may scratch your furniture when he feels neglected. (A negative reaction is sometimes better than neglect.) Provide him with more attention in order to prevent mischief.

Keep your cat's claws trimmed so they don't become caught in your carpet. You might even opt for a commercial carpet, made for outdoor use, that is attractive but claw proof. There are also indoor carpets that are rugged and very cat-friendly. You might want to apply this carpet to a section or entire wall so your cat can have his own wall to romp on.

Try to purchase furniture that a cat won't feel was designed for him to scratch, such as pieces covered in scratchy, nubby fabrics, or leather. Usually a smooth or velvety fabric isn't enticing.

If your furniture is so fragile and valuable that the mere touch of your cat's claws will destroy it, you may opt to section off the area with a sturdy decorative screen that your cat can't push aside or climb. Another strategy is to put all these pieces in one or more rooms and don't give your cat access. After all, claws are more important than space and many a cat lives and thrives in a small apartment.

It's best to provide your cat with cat-friendly scratching resources at the start. Therefore, if you decide to redecorate one day, your cat will still have his own means for pedicures and exercise. But just to be safe, I would give him new objects to scratch so he's sure to be distracted from your new furnishings.

Don't compromise your cat's claws. He's proud of them because they are a large part of his identity.

Soft Paws

You're about to redecorate and you want to be sure your cat doesn't carry on a destruction derby with your new furniture. One of your friends had Soft Paws put on her cats' paws by the veterinarian. Soft Paws are hard plastic caps that cover a cat's nails. Soft Paws are not permanent and have to be replaced every few months. Perhaps these would be the answer to your present dilemma.

If your cat is the mellow not-a-care-in-the-world type, Soft Paws might be the answer. But a high-energy, thin-skinned cat may become agitated. If the cat isn't cooperative the Soft Paws must be glued to a cat's paws under anesthesia, which adds another element of potential stress. This stress could result in deviant behavior. Your cat also might remove the Soft Paws through sheer perseverance and force. Fortunately, a cat doesn't usually harm himself by removing them.

Most cats prefer to have unencumbered feet. I've found that a cat usually has a low tolerance for things that restrain or modify his natural locomotion. If your cat's veterinarian does recommend Soft Paws, make certain you know all the pros and cons before you have them applied. Instead, why don't you try the cat-friendly alternatives given in this chapter.

EXERCISE

An outdoor cat enjoys his freedom, adventure, and great physical workouts. The downside is that his life span is frequently short. An outdoor cat is vulnerable to numerous kinds of catastrophes, such as cars, fights with dogs or other cats, mischievous children, and anticat people. Letting him outdoors is a gamble. If you can accept and live with that, fine! If not, there are things you can do to provide recreational exercise and adventure for an indoor cat. An indoor cat is dependent on you.

Inspirations for Indoor Activity

An indoor cat can be motivated to motion with something as simple as a ball of aluminum foil, a cork, or a pipe cleaner. But make certain he doesn't try to swallow any of these.

A box or paper shopping bag provides a favorite source of fun—he can jump in and out or use it as a spot for sneak attacks on his companion. An empty grocery bag or box on the floor will provide a spot for your cat to hang out in. (If you use a shopping bag, be sure to snip off the handles so his head can't be caught in them.) When your cat is in the box or bag, dangle a string or one of his toys nearby so he can go for it. New spots such as these can add a whole new dimension to his play.

The commercial Kitty Tease and Cat Dancer toys are marvelous means of exercise. Many cats will bring these to you in their mouths—a hint that they want you to play. Others will drag them around for amusement. There's a Cat Dancer with a fake bird on the end that's a real attention getter. These toys are available in most pet supply stores and from mail order sources. You also might prefer to make your own. (See *Create Your Cat's Toys*, page 40.)

Many a cat is a fanatical retriever and bedtime is their prime time to play fetch. At this time the cat knows his people are captive. They're relaxed, in a fixed position, and he has their undivided attention. All he has to do is persist. They're not about to budge.

A cat sometimes chooses to exercise on the top of a television. In between snoozes he may dangle his head and paws and swish his tail over the screen. The heat of the television and the movement and reflections on the screen are the attraction. Nature programs are usually a hit. This may seem to provide no exercise for your cat, but for the couch potato cat, this is a great way to get a bit more physically fit.

Your cat might like to chase imaginary objects or even his own tail. He creates his own stimulation and gets some exercise in turn.

If you have one cat, a companion cat can become his exercise buddy. Together, most cats will romp, chase, and wrestle. An athletic companion can become your sedentary cat's role model.

Some cats are fascinated by shadows or rays of reflected light on the wall or floor and they will chase them with great enthusiasm. You can simulate reflected light with a flashlight or a commercial laser light that is available at most pet supply shops.

Some cats will chase soap bubbles.

Create Your Cat's Toys

I have found the following toys to be very cat-friendly because they are not harmful. Most cats are challenged by them.

CATNIP TOYS

Commercial catnip toys don't always entice cats. If your cat's a catnip fan, you can make catnip toys in various whimsical shapes.

- scissors
- felt or wool fabric scraps
- needle and thread
- catnip and teaspoon
- tissue paper or fabric scraps

1. Cut fabric into 5-inch shapes, such as fish, cat faces, hearts, suns, moons, or whatever shape pleases you. Cut two of each shape. If you like, you can add embroidered details such as a happy face, a sun, or the whiskers on a cat face.

2. Place like pieces together, right sides together. Sew the pieces together about ½ inch from the edge, leaving an opening of about 1 inch. A sewing machine will speed up the process, but you can sew these by hand.

3. Turn the toy inside out.

4. Spoon ⅓ teaspoon or more catnip into the opening.

5. Stuff the toy full with tissue paper or fabric scraps. The tissue paper will make fascinating crinkly noises when your cat touches the toy. If your cat prefers floppy toys, use less stuffing.

6. Sew up the opening and sprinkle a touch more catnip on the outside.

7. If you like, for even more cat fun, wrap the toy in tissue paper so your cat can open his own gift.

If there's any chance your cat may chew and eat the toy, supervise his play to avoid a catastrophe. Instead of sewing the toy closed, you could use Velcro, so you can refill the toy with fresh catnip—that is, if the toy isn't demolished first.

KITTY LURE

This is a cat-friendly toy of intrigue that will sway and turn at your cat's touch.

- 25-inch-long round curtain rod or plastic or wooden wand
- thick cord

1. Attach cord to rod or pole by wrapping cord around end of pole and tying in a secure knot.
2. Dangle a favorite toy securely at end of cord. Make sure you fasten the toy by knotting it to end of cord.

You can make any additions or variations that will entice your cat.

BOUNCY CAT LURE

- wire hanger
- crumpled felt

1. Straighten out hanger so it forms a long, crooked curvy rod.
2. Attach pieces of felt to the ends.
3. Bend hanger so it forms quarter or semicircle.

Jiggle it and your cat will soon appear to check it out. If your cat is relentless in his passion for the kitty lure or bouncy cat lure, attach it to a ceiling hook, the back of a rocker, or any spot where it will be stable but retain its motion. If the cord isn't long enough for your cat to reach, position hook over a bed or chair. This may give you a respite from constant play. If your cat is somewhat clumsy, a rocker may not work.

Games with Your Cat

Many cats prefer to have their people included in their play. This is an honor, so keep this in mind if your cat seeks you out. You might include the following games into his repertoire of capers.

An aluminum foil ball, felt mouse, or crumpled wad of paper can be the object of a game of "toss and fetch." Most cats learn to play this game when they're kittens, and it's probably related to their hunting instinct. They frequently prefer to offer their catch as a gift to their person. To reinforce this game, praise your cat after he fetches and follow up with another toss. If the game goes on too long, divert your cat's attention with a romp on the scratching post.

Your cat might also like to play with a sock that contains catnip. It can be divided or sectioned off by string to become an interesting and fun shape.

Initiate a game of hide-and-seek by chasing him behind a piece of furniture. Quickly run to another room, hide yourself, and call him. It's your enthusiasm that will inspire him. Remain silent until he discovers you, then congratulate him and start to run after him. Stop abruptly so he can make his getaway. Take a while to find him.

Your cat might love to be tossed up in the air. This expends energy for the two of you. But be sure you're precise in your catch.

If you live in an apartment building, your cat might enjoy strolls in the hall. Accompany him, or leave the door open so he can return at will if it's safe for him to venture alone. Be sure to provide him with a collar and tag whether he strolls alone or accompanied.

Don't be surprised if your cat joins you in your exercise program. He may love to be held in your arms as you run on your treadmill, or your exercise may simply inspire him to run and romp.

Remember to be enthusiastic and perky when you play with your cat. Otherwise your boredom and lethargy may be contagious. Your cat needs challenge to have fun. Don't think you can hide your feelings from him.

Outdoor Jaunts for Indoor Cats

If you're determined to take your cat on an outdoor foray, the following preparations will make it easier:

1. Furnish your cat with a kitty harness so he doesn't stage a Houdini escape. A kitty harness is a nylon figure eight that wraps around the cat's shoulders and under his forelegs. It can be purchased from a local pet supply store. Don't use a collar and leash. The collar can cause him to choke if he pulls on the leash.

2. Acquaint him with the harness indoors first. Give him a treat before you put on the harness so he builds up a positive association. Repetition will reinforce this association.

3. Put your cat in his carrier or wrap him in a towel for his introductory walk so you can carry him out with ease.

4. Take him outside at a quiet time of day, in a secluded spot, away from street noises.

If he's still wary and frightened after a few trips, let him be a window gazer. Many an indoor cat loses his yen for going outdoors. Older cats may especially opt for "home sweet home."

MOVING WITH YOUR CAT

Country Cat Moves to the City

An avid country cat, who has always adored the great outdoors, can adapt to an apartment in the big city with careful planning. If you feel it would be too traumatic for your cat to make such an adjustment, find a home for him within or near his favorite turf or in a suburban locale. But be certain the new people can offer your cat the attention he needs. Some of these suggestions may also be used to spice up any indoor cat's daily agenda.

You might want to start off with two litter boxes in your new apartment so he feels indulged.

If your cat's an athlete, furnish your new digs with a floor-to-ceiling cat tree, condo, or scratching post and a variety of smaller accessories. Create a sunny corner for him to claim.

A kitty porch is a cat-friendly item that can be attached to an appropriate window so your cat can get a whiff and view of the outdoors in a small enclosed space. It usually consists of a wooden perch enclosed by screening. Such an item is available by mail order if you can't find it at your local pet supply shop. (Refer to *Cat Fancy* or another cat magazine.)

If your cat is a single cat, a new companion could spice up his life (see Chapter 8). However, if you have several cats and your new home will be much smaller than your previous one, create numerous spots for each cat to have privacy and/or rotate areas with each other at will. The greater the selection the better. You might even provide a couple of window seats. They may all choose to hang out in the same spot, but let that be their decision.

City Cat Moves to the Country

You want to introduce your city cat to the great outdoors. This may be quite a jolt for him, even if he's a mover and a shaker. The following tips will ease the transition and can also be applied to any indoor cat's introduction to the great outdoors.

If your cat has not yet been neutered or spayed, he or she should be at least two weeks before the move to the country. Make certain all his vaccinations are up to date, especially rabies (which can be contracted through the bite of a rabid animal).

Before you let him outside, you should both be settled

in your new home. You want your cat to become well acquainted and comfortable with the interior layout so he's not overwhelmed by too many new surroundings. Once your cat is indoor savvy, you can start to take him out for short outings—preferably on leash wearing a kitty harness.

Make sure your cat always wears a safety collar that has an elastic insert that allows him to slip out of the collar if it's caught on something. Attach an identification tag or write your name, address, and phone number to the collar.

There are organizations that will tattoo a number on the inside of your cat's ear. Your cat will have to be anesthetized for the procedure, but the tattoo is permanent. Many a lost cat has been united with his owner thanks to this tattoo. An ID microchip is also available. It is implanted in the cat's ear under anesthesia. Most veterinary offices or shelters have information available on this device and procedure. Many lost cats are identified by these devices.

The installation of a commercial cat door will provide easy access for your cat. If other animals intrude, you can provide your cat with a special collar and cat door that are electronically matched so your cat is the only animal able to go through the door.

For safety's sake and to reduce your own anxiety, feed your cat each evening just before sunset. That will provide the impetus for him to be home before dark and at that time you can close his cat door.

After your cat has had several supervised jaunts, you can let him go out unsupervised. Start him off slowly—maybe an hour the first several times. Make absolutely certain he knows how to gain quick entrance when he wants to return indoors in a hurry. You can condition your cat to return home with the offer of a special treat or his favorite game. Use a whistle or shake a box of cat food to attract him. If you praise and engage him when he appears, this will become a happy habit.

YOUR CAT, THE HUNTER

It's a natural urge for an outdoor cat to pursue a bird. Because a cat has become such a domesticated animal and is so adaptable, it is easy for us to forget that he is also a born hunter. He will instinctively hunt whatever moves and catch whatever he can get. A cat may not always devour his prey, which appears to be cruel. This could be because his appetite is already satiated and because his urge to hunt is for sport as well as food. But this is inherent in a cat's nature. If something moves in front of him, he's challenged and will not stop to tell himself he's not hungry. Instead, he will pursue the chase to the finish.

If your cat presents you with his catch, you may become overcome with grief or anger. But he doesn't know that you don't relish or even plan to eat his catch. This is his gift to you to win your praise and esteem and to show that he's the very best cat. You'll confuse him if you yell or punish him. Try to swallow your dismay and think of it as your cat's gift to you.

These pointers will help you to cope with your cat's hunting:

1. Don't tempt your cat by putting bird feeders on your property.
2. Don't put out food for any animals that could be potential prey.
3. Attach a bell to your cat's collar and hope the ring will precede his spring.
4. Don't lose your control if your cat presents you with a dead mouse or bird. Breathe deeply and try not to scream at your cat, which will only add to the hysteria. Remember that a cat is an animal and motivated primarily by his instincts.

5. Distract your cat if he presents you with a bird or mouse that is still alive. Lure him away with his favorite toy or some food, put him in the house, and quickly return to help his victim. You may need to seek medical attention. If the animal he's caught is fatally wounded, dispose of it in the proper receptacle if you don't choose to bury it.

6. If you don't want your cat to eat his catch, pick it up in newspaper or a plastic bag and carry it away to a secluded spot. But this is not advisable because it could be a source of disease.

Although it is possible for a cat to be raised with a bird or rabbit that he won't treat as prey, this is a result of domestic circumstances. Your cat can be taught to interact amicably with a household bird or rabbit, but outdoors he's driven by his natural instincts.

Remember, if your cat does hunt, he can possibly contract worms from his catch. His stool should be checked every few months so worm medication can be administered if necessary.

"His therapist says he needs a hobby."

Sexual Maturity and Pregnancy

MALE CATS

You've decided to adopt a male cat. You wonder when and if he'll have to be neutered. Maybe it would be fun to have him intact! Generally the surgery should be performed when a male has just reached sexual maturity. This can be as early as five and a half months or as late as one year. Within the past several years there have been studies done to indicate that a healthy male kitten can be neutered safely at three or four months without any physical problems. Many shelters adhere to this practice to reduce the number of intact males that lead to homeless kittens.

Symptoms of Male Sexual Maturity

The signs of sexual maturity in a male cat are usually a macho aggressive quality, random howls, and posturing, such as a puffed tail, flattened ears, and an arched back. You may notice him constantly trying to dart out any open window or door. His demeanor with you and any companion cat may become remarkably rough. He may develop a ravenous appetite that is a result of high hormonal levels. If your male cat doesn't exhibit any of these signs at the age of one year, I suggest you consult your veterinarian.

TOMCAT SCENT

Tomcat is the term for an intact, or unaltered, male. The scent of a tomcat's urine can be very potent and even unbearable in some instances. Your male cat's urine will usually take on a stronger aroma when he reaches sexual maturity.

A sexually mature male may start to "christen" any object he pleases to mark his territory. When the urge is present, he will back against such an object, raise his tail in the air, and begin to urinate. His high sexual energy may cause him to spray frequently. This activity may not be limited to his litter box—even if he's previously always been on target.

The tomcat scent is very persistent. Even though you've cleaned the area thoroughly, your cat may still detect his scent and rechristen this area, along with new ones. To prevent or stop indiscriminate urination, or spraying around, it is best to have your male neutered when his urine and tomcat behavior become offensive. (See also Chapter 11.)

Should You Neuter?

A sexually mature intact male who goes outdoors may fight with other male cats. The fights may involve defending his territory from another tom or competing for a female in heat.

A street tom's life can be one continuous battle for food, shelter, and sex. The average life span of a street tom is not even a year. A house cat with outdoor privileges may fare better than a street tom, but even his existence is iffy.

In contrast, a neutered male who goes outdoors is not usually filled with that macho go-get-'em instinct. He won't be interested in females in heat. He will have enough energy to defend himself or to elude the invader if threatened.

Sometimes a person may take pride in his or her tomcat's bravado and scars. But as the tom ages, his ability to conquer will diminish as he confronts younger toms. Aside from brawls, a tom can become lost as he may wander far from home in his pursuit of a female. He also may leave many a female with a family. This is tragic because our present homeless kitten population is enormous. Street-born kittens rarely get a chance to be adopted.

An indoor tom may not experience the traumas of an outdoor tom, but his high hormonal levels usually cause him to be agitated and may cause him to urinate throughout your house.

NEUTERING AND SPRAYING

A neutered male will usually revert to the clean litter box habits he had as a kitten, and spraying will diminish ten days to two weeks after the surgery. If an older male is neutered, it may take a while longer for his urine to lose the tomcat odor. He may be more apt to spray if overstimulated. Lysol and a sweet-smelling shampoo should defuse the scent. If these products don't do the trick, you can purchase one of the commercial scent eliminators in liquid or spray form that are available from your cat's veterinarian or a pet store. Evsco Pharmaceuticals makes a spray called the Equalizer, which is a very effective stain and odor eliminator.

Sometimes a female hormone is prescribed to curb

spraying, but extensive use of hormones can trigger physical problems and is not always effective.

A neutered cat will sometimes spray as a result of overstimulation. He becomes worked up and releases his feelings or energy in a spray. This may be a signal to you to give him more attention or to change something in his daily agenda. If you're stumped, you may need some professional behavioral in-depth consultation to remedy the situation.

RETAINED TESTICLE

Sometimes one of the testicles doesn't descend when a male kitten reaches maturity. This condition is called cryptorchidism. When such a male cat is neutered, the veterinarian must search out and remove the testicle that hasn't descended.

If the veterinarian doesn't do exploratory surgery to locate and remove the undescended testicle, the cat's person should be well informed of the potential consequences. A male will still be a tomcat for as long as he has the testicle. He will probably continue to spray, and the urine have an offensive odor.

Sometimes your vet can determine if he's still intact by the look of the male's penis. There are also cases where neither testicle descends and exploratory surgery is necessary to locate the testicles.

SEX AND THE NEUTERED MALE

Occasionally an altered male cat may mount the female and bite her neck. If the female is intact and in heat, chances are the neutered male will end up with a case of stress-related cystitis from his supreme efforts and the female with a case of unrequited passion. Sometimes neutered males also mimic the mating ritual with each other.

NEUTERED MALES AND TOMCATS

Unfamiliar tomcats can cause emotional and physical stress to a neutered male. It's not uncommon for an alien tomcat to appear at a window or on a lawn and wreak havoc with the resident cat. The resident cat will often be excited and stressed. If the tomcat sprays urine on the altered cat's territory, the resident cat may try to match it with his own. Your cat may also end up with a mild bladder spasm or even a full-blown case of cystitis from the trauma.

If your cat and the interloper start to fight outdoors, break up the confrontation by spritzing the cats with water from a plant mister or the garden hose, or douse them with a bucket of water. Do not attempt to pick up your cat or—worse yet—the strange tom. You could get severely scratched.

If the alien tomcat continues to make guest appearances and you can't get rid of him, do any of the following:

1. Distract your cat by luring him with food into a room where he can't see the tomcat.

2. Locate the tomcat's care-giver and diplomatically suggest that it would be advantageous to have him neutered. Offer to take care of the cost if all else fails.

3. If the tomcat is homeless, arrange to have him neutered. A humane trap may be needed to catch him if the tom is feral. Many a homeless cat has secured a home through this route.

PHYSICAL PROBLEMS OF THE UNNEUTERED MALE

An intact male is vulnerable to cystitis and obstructed bladder. Cystitis is an inflammation in the bladder, whereas an obstruction occurs when the urinary passage is completely blocked and the cat is unable to urinate. He may stress and strain but only produce a few drops. The bladder swells as far as it can. The pressure causes the kidneys to shut down, which results in a condition known as uremia. Quick help is of the essence or the condition will be fatal.

For treatment the cat is usually hospitalized. The obstruction is relieved and treatment is given if uremia is present. For days the cat's condition can be touch and go. Castration will usually be recommended.

The recurrence of urinary attacks is less common in a neutered cat. But once a male's bladder is sensitized, it becomes more vulnerable. If it is under much stress, the bladder may suffer, although the attacks will decline following neutering.

A urethrostomy is a surgical procedure where the end of the urethra is removed, including the penis, to widen the opening to prevent blockage caused by stones or crystals. With this surgery, chances are greater than 90 percent that there won't be obstructions. Foods are forever changing because of more recent findings, so check with your cat's veterinarian for foods that won't irritate the bladder. The surgery provides a wider opening for the bladder, but it doesn't eliminate any problems that can occur with an inappropriate diet.

Vasectomy as an Alternative to Neutering

A vasectomy is a surgical procedure where the tube that carries the sperm from the testis is severed. The testicles are not removed. This procedure prevents conception but doesn't rid a cat of the male hormones that urge him to spray.

After a vasectomy a male cat will also retain all of his macho tomcat characteristics.

FEMALE CATS

You just saw the most terrific female kitten at your local shelter. She's two months old and such a love. You were told that they may spay her (remove her ovaries and uterus) before she's adopted. This really surprised you because you were under the impression it was best for a cat to reach sexual maturity before being spayed or neutered. Is this unusual?

Kittens and cats are now being neutered and spayed before reaching sexual maturity—especially at shelters. This is to help halt the current population explosion of homeless kittens. If a kitten is spayed or neutered before adoption, breeding is prevented. Many veterinarians have not experienced any problems with this practice, and if the anesthesia is very carefully monitored, a kitten fares very well and recovers quickly from surgery. But the common practice is still to spay and neuter when a cat reaches sexual maturity. There are ways to determine when your cat has reached sexual maturity.

Symptoms of Female Sexual Maturity

A female usually reaches sexual maturity between five and a half months and a year of age. Sexual maturity is usually signaled by her first "heat," or estrus. Each cat's cycle differs, but a "heat" can last for three or four days. If a female has cysts on her ovaries, she may go in and out of heat repeatedly.

Although sometimes a cat is silent during her first heat, usually the initial heat is an extravaganza. The female becomes very vocal with a touch of a frustrated lyric soprano. She may become sensitive along her lower back, so that her rear shoots up into the air when she's stroked. Don't be surprised if she crouches low to the ground, moans softly, and rolls back and forth on the floor. Such posture helps to relieve the uncomfortable sensation she feels inside. If a female's heats are silent, it is usually safe to assume she's reached sexual maturity by eight months old.

It's not uncommon for a female to urinate and defecate in places other than the litter box to bring attention to her condition. But her normal toilet habits will usually return several days after she goes out of heat. She should be spayed soon or this behavior may resume.

A cat's appetite may also plummet when she's in heat.

Should You Spay?

If a female cat who becomes sexually mature isn't spayed, she's a target for the unspayed syndrome, which can leave a female vulnerable to serious physical and emotional disorders. Recurrent heats are both stressful and bothersome for the female and person.

POTENTIAL PHYSICAL PROBLEMS

1. Cystic ovaries—When a female comes into heat and the egg produced in the ovary is not released, cystic ovaries can occur. They can cause recurrent heats, which can be critical.

2. Pyometra—a severe infection of the uterus. It is the result of hormonally induced changes in the uterus that allow secondary infection to occur. Excessive secretions may accumulate in the uterus, which provides an environment conducive for bacteria to grow.

   Loss of appetite, lethargy, and bladder problems may be symptoms of pyometra. These problems can occur concurrently or independently. The *treatment* is to remove the ovaries and uterus.

3. Unless the female is bred every time she comes into estrus, she won't ovulate (she only ovulates after coitus). Her hormones can become unbalanced, and she becomes a vulnerable target for illness.

4. Breast tumors—The cancer usually manifests itself in the form of breast tumors, which may be discovered when the cat's person feels lumps in the cat's breast. The veterinarian subsequently diagnoses them as benign or malignant.

   The cancer is treated with surgery and medication or solely medication. Either treatment should be combined with positive support therapy from the cat's owner. The prognosis depends on the severity of the tumors. There are cats that survive comfortably for months. Others do well for years. For some unfortunate ones time is very short.

Don't gamble with your female's health. Unless she is bred every time she has a heat, she can endure an immeasurable amount of emotional and physical stress. An ovariohysterectomy will prevent this unnecessary stress.

POTENTIAL EMOTIONAL PROBLEMS

The emotional stress from a female's pent-up sexual energy can affect her catsonality—often dramatically. Because she is uncomfortable and frustrated, her stress tolerance is lowered and she is easily threatened. With a succession of heats, she becomes even more fragile, and her behavior may become unpredictable. If she becomes anxious or excited, she may lash out at her people or feline companions in self-defense. She might try to stop them from an activity that's too high in energy for her with a sudden swipe, nip, hiss, or all three. Her aggressive behavior is her response to fear, and if she continues to feel threatened, such behavior can become unacceptable. Because the female can't cope, she may become truly out of control. This extreme tension and defensive behavior would not be so intense if the female had been spayed. Her catsonality would be the same, but she would be more trusting and easier to live with.

FEMALE'S SENSUALITY

The female's sensuality is not violated by an ovariohysterectomy. Once the female is sexually mature, her hormones have already triggered the area of the brain that controls her femininity. (There are those who feel that a female's sensuality is firmly established even before sexual maturity.) Her behavior continues to be controlled by her highly developed senses. Many a female cat becomes more sensual and affectionate after she is spayed because she feels emotionally and physically more comfortable.

DON'T BELITTLE YOUR CAT

Once your female is spayed, don't refer to her as "it." She can sense your disdain and discomfort and it can cause her *dis*-ease. Remember that your cat is very much affected by your treatment of her.

SELF-ABUSE

An unspayed female will sometimes scratch and bite various parts of her body. This behavior can be triggered by her heats. If this is her way of externalizing her condition, this habit declines and eventually ceases after she is spayed. She may need some particular medical treatment and supplement to her diet. The veterinarian will address this after her surgery. An underlying respiratory ailment, such as asthma or a cardiac problem, may be the primary source of discomfort or stress, and her skin becomes her secondary source of stress. A thorough physical examination can determine if there is such a problem.

SILENT HEATS

When a female doesn't externalize her heats, it's not uncommon for her person to see no apparent reason to have her spayed. Unfortunately, an unspayed cat is an ideal target for cancer because of the emotional and physical stress.

PERIODIC LITTERING

An intact female may exhibit no classic signs of estrus. But she may periodically avoid her litter box. This is a signal of discomfort. Schedule an appointment with the veterinarian to have her examined.

CYSTITIS

An unspayed female is under a greater amount of emotional stress. Although diet is also a factor in cystitis, stress can greatly affect your cat's health. When she becomes anxious, the effects of her anxiety can affect her bladder if it is one of her stress targets. This, in turn, may trigger bouts of cystitis (inflammation of the bladder). Symptoms include straining in the litter box, and the cat's urine may appear bloody. A spayed female is less prone to cystitis attacks.

SUDDEN DISCORD

After her hospital stay, your cat's scent may be unfamiliar to any other cats you have at home. This could cause them to mistake her for an alien cat and strike out at her. Her post-op discomfort and anxiety may also trigger conflict. If there is any continued friction, separate the cats until you feel they will welcome each other's company, but the more relaxed you are, the calmer your cats will be. Your female may choose to be reclusive, but let her know you're available to nurture her. The following steps will also help avoid cat spats:

1. Remove your cat from her carrier and allow the other cats to go inside and get a whiff. A sprinkle of catnip in the carrier may sweeten the mix.
2. If the carrier is not feasible, rub your female with a towel and then rub that towel on your other cat or cats so the alien scent is transferred.

A spayed female may suddenly become agitated with a young intact female companion. Chances are the latter is in the midst of a silent heat that the spayed companion senses. The high energy upsets her and makes her tense, causing her to either ignore or hiss at her younger companion. An appointment should be scheduled to spay the young cat so their tense relationship doesn't become permanent.

You and your cat will enjoy a happier and healthier relationship if your cat is spayed. It's up to you to look after your cat's welfare.

Spaying

PREPARATIONS FOR THE OVARIOHYSTERECTOMY

The female should receive a clean bill of health from the veterinarian before her ovariohysterectomy, in which the ovaries and uterus are removed. If only the uterus is removed, the female can't become pregnant but can still go into heat.

Before you go to the veterinarian, you must physically and emotionally prepare your cat for the surgery. Include one or two of her belongings in her carrier for her security objects while she's hospitalized. You should also inquire about the continuation of any medication that your cat may be presently on.

AT THE VET'S

Your cat usually will stay at the veterinary hospital for one to three days. Although this seems like a long time, the surgery is straightforward and uncomplicated. Her incision will be either on her side or, most commonly, on the abdomen.

YOUR FEMALE'S POSTOPERATIVE CARE

Make certain you follow any directions that your veterinarian gives you. The veterinarian will give you instructions regarding food and water. Normally, wait at least two hours before you feed your female. Water should be provided sparingly the first day, and don't give your cat any rich or unfamiliar food.

Cat acrobatics shouldn't be encouraged, and don't let your cat go outdoors.

If the incision becomes red or swollen and she licks it incessantly, have her incision checked. If she only occasionally licks at the sutures, distract her with catnip or affection. Phone the vet if there's any increased tenderness or swelling around the suture line. Dissolving sutures are generally used in surgery. If not, the sutures are usually easily and painlessly removed by the veterinarian or a technician within ten to fourteen days.

If your cat appears depressed, lethargic or anorexic for more than one day, contact the veterinarian.

If your cat should exhibit estrus symptoms, that may be indicative of a retained ovary or ovarian tissue. Contact your vet. Exploratory surgery may be needed.

Common Misconceptions About Spaying Your Female Cat

Fiction: A female cat will become lazy after she is spayed. She won't want to exercise and will become totally lethargic.

Fact: After the surgery, her hormonal level is lower, so she usually becomes more relaxed. Her energy level isn't as high. Although an outdoor cat may be less affected than an indoor cat, you may want to put some extra effort into playing with your spayed cat to make sure she gets enough exercise. You can inspire her activity if she isn't self-motivated by taking her for walks around the house, chasing her around, or bringing home a companion.

Fiction: She will concentrate only on food and become a blimp.

Fact: This will be true only if your cat continues to eat the same amount of food as she did before her surgery. A spayed cat won't need as much food as before her surgery. If she starts to become too hefty, feed her smaller amounts of food.

Fiction: A cat knows when to stop eating.

Fact: The number of chubby and obese cats indicates otherwise. This notion may be true of a cat in her natural environment, but is not accurate for domestic cats.

Fiction: A female's sensuality will disappear after she's spayed.

Fact: A cat's sensuality is not dependent on her sexual organs. It's been my experience that if a cat is spayed at sexual maturity, she has already reached full femininity and is not in need of further hormone stimulation. Therefore, a cat's sensuality doesn't vanish after surgery. If you decided to have your cat spayed or neutered before sexual maturity, consult your veterinarian for his particular experience and viewpoint.

Fiction: The female can have heats after she's spayed.

Fact: The female can exhibit heat symptoms if she has retained ovarian tissue. In such a case, exploratory surgery is performed to locate and remove the retained tissue, or a blood test will be done to determine if she has a high estrogen level. Although the test isn't always conclusive, a high estrogen level would indicate she may still be intact.

BREEDING, PREGNANCY, AND KITTEN CARE

Breeding a Female Cat

To breed or not to breed a female cat should be a thoughtful, careful decision. The female's basic body structure, general health, and resistance to disease are important aspects to consider. You must be able to deal with the responsibility of a pregnant cat who will very soon become a nursing mother with kittens. The kittens will be filled with disruptive energy. Your home will become a mini kitten adoption center. Your economic obligation will skyrocket, especially if the mother or kittens need extensive medical care.

You feel you can deal with the above factors, but you must be committed to your decision. Millions of homeless cats and kittens are executed. Stray cats often die a slow, painful death on the streets. Do you want to add to this population? You may think you have all the kittens spoken for until, one by one, potential adopters drop out. You fantasize and think you could keep all of the litter, but this may not be so practical a solution. Breeding your cat can, indeed, be a wonderful and worthwhile experience, but be sure you have thoroughly considered your risks and responsibilities before you decide to go ahead.

EXOTIC BREEDS

If the female is of an exotic breed and a *particularly excellent specimen* of her breed, it *may* be acceptable to breed her. But remember, this is an involved process and can be extremely time-consuming, expensive, and also a *potential health risk* for your cat.

ABORTION

If you decide you do not want to take responsibility for a litter of kittens but your cat becomes pregnant anyway, you may choose to abort her. It's generally safe to abort a pregnant female if she is under six weeks pregnant and otherwise healthy. A competent veterinarian can abort and spay her.

Sometimes after the surgery a female's breasts can become very swollen. Although normally, removal of the ovaries and uterus eliminates the hormonal stimulation for breast development and milk production, some cats have a paradoxical reaction and the process continues. It is usually only a matter of a couple of weeks before the breasts return to normal.

CARE DURING PREGNANCY AND DELIVERY

Your cat's gestation period will probably range from sixty-four to sixty-nine days. During the first half of pregnancy she should continue to eat normally. But during the last three weeks of pregnancy the mother's normal food intake should be increased by a half. A good multivitamin and mineral supplement should also be added. Pregnant and nursing cats need high levels of calcium, so make sure her diet includes milk products or give her calcium pills. Your veterinarian may have some specific recommendations.

During her pregnancy don't be surprised if your expectant mama's catsonality has a radical change. Chances are she'll become very affectionate. She also may have a preference for a particular drawer or the bottom of a closet. You may want to line a sturdy basket or box with clean towels and set it up in a spot that is warm and quiet.

Your female may want you to stay with her while she gives birth. Her signal will be to cry out to you or attract your attention by running after you. If she wants your company, think calmly and speak softly so she is comforted by your presence. As she goes about her birthing, sit quietly nearby and assist only if she has difficulty. You can expect her to take charge of the entire process.

Consult your veterinarian before her delivery for some specific pointers and who you might call if she has a difficult labor, in case he or she is unreachable. Don't hesitate to phone for help if your female appears to be in distress. Sometimes it is necessary to perform a cesarean surgery if the mother is incapacitated.

After the mother gives birth, feed her as much food as you gave her during pregnancy or even more. Her weight and number of kittens will be your guide. Don't be surprised if she eats two or three times her normal amount. A nursing mother can be ravenous.

Caring for Kittens and Arranging for Adoption

The kittens should remain with the mother until they are at least six to eight weeks old unless her milk becomes depleted and she can't nurse them. You can prevent the mother from becoming depleted by monitoring her nutrition and separating her from the kittens from time to time.

She will probably need extra multivitamin and mineral supplements. (Seek medical advice if in doubt.)

If the mother's milk dries up, KMR (Kitten Milk Replacement) can be used as a substitute.

WEANING THE KITTENS

The kittens can start to eat solid food, yet continue to nurse, at four weeks old. But if they insist on nursing and ignore regular food, don't rush their weaning as long as the mother is in good health. If the mother is malnourished or sick, separate her from her kittens until they are ready to be adopted.

Provide separate bowls so that the more timid kittens have the best chance of getting their share. The dominant kittens may try to push their timid littermates out of the way. Monitor their feedings and arrange for the timid kittens to eat separately if needed. Keep a damp washcloth handy for the kittens who bathe in their food.

The mother takes care of the kittens' wastes in their early stages. Later on she will teach them to use the litter box. (See Chapter 11.) If they are not always on target with the box, it may be a medical problem such as worms or diet.

WHY ARE THE KITTENS UNLIKE THE MOTHER?

The kittens' dispositions are only partial reflections of the mother's catsonality. There are other factors, such as genetic characteristics from the father, which affect her litter's temperaments. If the female was an outdoor cat, more than one male could have fathered her litter. The female can ovulate a number of times during heat. If inseminated by different males each time, she can produce a litter with multiple sires.

MAMA CAT'S LIB

The mother cat may ignore her kittens if she doesn't have the energy or inclination to care for them. Not every female has the emotional and physical resources to be a blue-ribbon mother. So you may become the surrogate mom and be in charge of caring for their physical and emotional needs.

MALE CAT IN RESIDENCE

If you also have an intact male cat, he should be neutered very soon even if he is the proud father. A tomcat's energy level can often clash with the kittens' high energy and cause him to strike out at a kitten. Yes, there are exceptions. But, in general, a neutered male's stress tolerance is greater, allowing him to adapt more easily to the kittens. In many cases, it is better not to take the chance of having an intact tom in residence. If you are determined not to neuter your tom, you might want to confine the kittens to one room and prevent the tom from interacting with them.

A neutered male may ignore the kittens or be fascinated by them. A shy male cat can sometimes blossom in the presence of kittens. He may even allow the kittens to try to nurse from him when the mother is not around.

The mother can go into heat even while she is nursing the kittens. Each female cat has her own cycle but the most common occurrence of heat is twice a year. Avoid any potential matings by keeping any intact males away from her quarters.

Finally, a neutered male *may* still have the ability to impregnate an intact female for several months after he's neutered. This would apply to a tomcat that had a very high hormonal level before his neutering.

ADOPTION

If you decide to keep one of the kittens, observe the mother with her kittens to see which kitten is most dependent on her. This is the kitten to keep. Don't keep the entire litter unless you are quite certain that you can provide the essential care.

Try to place pairs of chummy kittens together, but if they must be separated try to send them to a home that has another cat or kitten in residence.

The more you interact with the kittens, the more socialized they will become. They will be able to transfer this acceptance and appreciation to their new caregivers.

Try to keep one kitten to ease the mother's loss if she is your only cat. Space the adoption of the rest of her litter so her anxiety isn't so great. Shower her with extra attention. Tell her how you will now have more time together and that her kittens are going to be just fine in their new homes. No, she probably will not understand your words, but she will respond to the positive feelings you express by your body language and in the tone of your voice. Her anxiety will be eased by your calm demeanor.

Emotions, Communication, and Your Cat

A CAT HAS FEELINGS

You never knew a cat had feelings until you lived with your first cat. It occurred to you that your cat clearly expressed emotions—happiness, rage, anxiety. Yes, cats are not people, but cats do have definite emotions that humans can recognize. Because a cat doesn't intellectualize or talk away the feelings, they are usually not internalized (as with humans), so it is not difficult to get a clear read of your cat's mood. You will notice, however, that your cat uses body language to express his feelings or emotions.

HAPPINESS

The easiest emotion to interpret is happiness. The most obvious expression of happiness is purring. Purring does not only indicate happiness—a cat can also purr out of fear or anxiety. Your cat may invite you to stroke her with a loud purr, suddenly become overstimulated, and a swat and hiss will accompany her purr. (See chart on emotions on pages 83–85.) The buildup of energy becomes too much and your cat becomes threatened.

Other expressions of happiness can be communicated by a cat's facial expressions. Some cats actually smile when they are happy. Their eyes take on a lovely glow, and the muscles in their face relax.

Happiness is also revealed through your cat's body language. When a cat is happy, his body is relaxed, his ears face forward, and his breathing is slow and gentle.

Bumping or nuzzling you is usually a sign of happiness. Your cat may bump his head or body against you when he's feeling happy. You can often measure how happy he is by the amount of pressure he exerts or the height of his jumps to reach a particular part of your body. He may be satisfied to just nuzzle his head against your hand or body to let you know when he feels good.

Contact is another way a cat reveals he's happy. Contact can be the source of his happiness, or his happiness can cause him to seek contact with people or animals. A cat may rest his paw against his person's arm, causing him to purr with this slight contact. He may lick his owner, nuzzle against him, or beg to have his head stroked. Any contact such as this adds to his happiness. Hovering or claiming is when your cat bumps his face against your legs or another part of your body. This action releases his scent (pheromones), which pleases him, and you become "his" territory.

However, a relaxed cat may not always want contact and may move away from your touch. There are times when a cat wants intimacy at a distance. He may prefer to set the boundaries.

Your Cat Can Drool When Happy

Not all cats are droolers, but your cat may be one. A feeling of happiness may stimulate his salivary glands, so he may begin to drool.

Your Cat May Knead or Lick

When a kitten nurses, he kneads his mother's breast as he sucks on her nipple. This satisfies his hunger and fills him with pleasure because it stimulates her milk release. This same motion may be carried into adulthood. A person's warm, comfortable body can inspire the kneading action that once brought such gratification. Your cat may knead because he's happy, or knead because he wants to become happy. He may also lick or suck your clothing or skin. If a kitten is separated from his mother too early, as an adult he may display these characteristics to such a degree that they become irksome.

DISCOURAGING A CAT WHO KNEADS AND SUCKS

If your cat's kneading and sucking bother you, you can take steps to break him of the habit. But remember—his kneading is an expression of his affection for you.

1. Try to distract your cat with a soft, cat-friendly object and praise him as he claims it.
2. Interest him in one of his favorite games.
3. Move to another room.
4. Sprinkle a bit of catnip on his scratching post to entice him to play with his post instead of you. This

diversion will also help to trim his nails—or be a reminder to you that he's due for a pedicure.

5. A baby pacifier or bottle nipple may satisfy the sucking or licking craving. Before you try any of these suggestions, rule out a diet deficiency with a physical checkup. And bear in mind that if his behavior is a nervous reaction to anxiety, abundant attention and/or a behavior-modification drug may be the remedy. (See Chapter 9.)

Unique Ways of Gaining Happiness

Your cat's pleasure may be a ride in the elevator, a tumble in the snow, a taste of pizza, a nap in the baby's crib, a snooze on your head, a munch of melon, a nature videotape, a box of tissue paper for a hideaway, or a perch on the highest ledge. A list of such pleasures is endless and differs for each cat.

ANXIETY

Because a cat is such an exquisitely sensitive creature, he's a prime target for anxiety. This is especially true of an indoor cat who is totally dependent on his person's behavior.

A cat experiences different kinds of anxiety. Fleeting anxiety is quickly discharged and not threatening. Prolonged anxiety and separation anxiety, on the other hand, if not immediately discharged, can turn into a pervasive fear or timidity, where a cat's peace of mind and physical well-being may be threatened.

Fleeting Anxiety

Your cat awaits his breakfast, but as you prepare it you're distracted by the television. He becomes uneasy and worried that he won't get his breakfast. His tail may flick, he may meow or rub up against your leg, or his body may ripple to indicate that he's anxious. As you pull yourself away from the television and return to him, his anxiety disappears. A cat may experience bouts of fleeting anxiety more than once during a typical day with no long-term ill effects.

Prolonged Anxiety

The presence of a new or alien cat, person, or other animal can trigger prolonged anxiety. For example, an unfamiliar houseguest who visits for a few days could cause your cat to become anxious. He might communicate it by withdrawal or fasting.

Your cat may also take his aggression out on an innocent companion cat or person, rather than on the one who agitated him.

Prolonged anxiety can also cause a cat to become unusually aggressive. If his anxiety is caused by an alien person or animal, he might actually attack. To his way of thinking, the new person or animal is the source of his anxiety and his reaction would be to strike against it. Even if your cat is anxious for reasons not related to a strange person or animal, he may strike out. An anxious cat may be likely to attack anything that moves because it adds to his anxiety.

PREVENT ATTACK-CAT SYNDROME

If a houseguest is a potential source of anxiety for your cat, sequester him from your visitor. Make sure the room you move him to is peaceful and contains all his creature comforts (food, water, litter box, toys, etc.). If he doesn't calm down and the anxiety-provoking situation lingers, a tranquilizer may be in order to help him through his anxiety bout. But remember that the tranquilizer is an auxiliary support. Your care and attention should be the primary source of help to increase his tolerance of stress. (See Chapter 9 for more information on difficult behavior.)

Aggressive Tendencies

An unneutered, sexually mature cat is more apt to become aggressive when anxious. His energy level is higher, which makes alien situations more threatening to him. It's also not uncommon for a cat who has had a traumatic time on the street or who has had multiple homes to have a difficult time coping with strange people, cats, and other animals.

There are also those cats who are worldly types and stress appears unknown to them. It's the particular cat's disposition or catsonality that determines how much stress he can comfortably integrate into his everyday life. But, typically, a cat is such a creature of habit that he'll instinctively resist change unless he seeks it out.

Familiarity

Your cat's familiarity with his daily patterns brings him a feeling of solid security. Any major—and sometimes even minor—change from what he knows can represent conflict and anxiety. His acceptance or lack of acceptance of the changes will depend on his self-esteem. His reactions can be unpredictable, but most situations can be resolved with time and patience. If your cat is a fragile creature, make it a point to introduce changes gently and gradually.

Separation Anxiety

Your cat may experience prolonged separation anxiety if he is left alone after he's become accustomed to more of your company. The absence of a companion cat could also disturb him. His anxiety may cause him to nibble at his food, withdraw, pout, vomit, or have a bout of cystitis. Your cat might even start to overgroom out of frustration and malaise. Arrange for someone to pop in and see him when you're detained and leave messages on your answering machine to reassure him if he has a positive reaction to your voice. But always remember to rule out a medical problem with a checkup or consultation with your vet.

LONG OR PERMANENT SEPARATION

Your cat could be deeply affected by a long or permanent separation, such as the loss of a companion cat or person. Emotional upset can many times trigger a medical problem. The degree to which your cat will be affected all hinges upon his stress tolerance and his constitution.

If you have lost a member of your household, you can help ease your cat's pain by treating yourself well. The more you can nurture yourself at home, the better your cat will feel. He'll respond to your good feelings. A daily bubble bath, meditation, or reading an inspiring book with him right beside you are a few things that might ease the pain.

MARITAL SPLIT

Immediate related emotional and/or physical problems in a cat can be triggered by the stress of a marital split. Generally, the cat's person or caregiver will experience much confusion and loss and perhaps later new feelings of independence or freedom. A cat may mirror these personality changes.

It's usually best for the cat to remain with the person with whom he interacts best. If there are two cats, they should stay together unless they've always seemed indifferent to each other. But if they must be parted, they will need substantial comforting to ease the separation anxiety.

After each cat has recovered from the separation and appears to have adapted to his new situation, a new companion cat would probably please him. (See Chapter 8 for more information.)

Drugs for Behavior Modification

Sometimes a cat's prolonged anxiety can't be allayed only by positive support from his people or companion cats. If there are undesirable behaviors, such as aggression, indiscriminate litter habits, or self-mutilation, auxiliary support must be given with pharmacological treatment. If the emotional problem has triggered a medical problem, both should be treated simultaneously. There are several drugs that are now prescribed for cats—each with different and similar properties. The most common are Valium (diazepam), BuSpar (buspirone), Elavil (amitriptyline), and Prozac (fluoxetine). I have found Valium to be most effective.

REACTIONS TO PSYCHOTROPIC DRUGS

These are drugs that are used extensively in humans for treatment of depression. Prozac is among the new antidepressants known as the SSRIs, or selective serotonin reuptake inhibitors. The SSRIs do not require periodic blood tests to monitor drug levels. Valium is a tranquilizer. Because of a cat's excellent muscle memory, which is especially retained and active when a cat experiences anxiety, Valium is effective because it relaxes the skeletal muscles. This is important for an anxious cat, but periodic blood tests are necessary to monitor drug levels, especially in the liver. In the past two decades, psychopharmacology has become quite sophisticated.

Herbals such as kava-kava, valerian, and St. John's wort are frequently used, with St. John's wort being the most investigated. The correct dosage is significant for effective treatment.

If your cat has a chronic problem, a drug, herbal, or homeopathic remedy will not always be the easy solution. A program of behavioral/emotional therapy is the answer. It's great when a drug can be a quick fix, but with a deeply rooted problem, a drug's effectiveness will diminish and the problem will reappear.

Reactions can vary with each drug. Your cat may become:

- Wobbly or ataxic within twenty minutes to an hour after the drug is given—This reaction sometimes lingers, to a much lesser degree, throughout the duration of the medication.

- Disoriented, chatter away, and try to resist the effects of the drug by running about.

- Hungry—You might want to modify your cat's diet if weight increase is an issue. (See Chapter 2.)

- Much more affectionate—A drug, such as Valium, relaxes the skeletal muscles. The more relaxed a cat's body is, the more receptive he is to contact.

- Lethargic and dazed—Such a reaction is not necessarily a bad thing, however, because it's important for his body to relax so he can learn to cope with confidence and sustain his emotional growth.

- More playful—This is a positive sign because it indicates that he is relaxed and his anxiety has started to wane.

REDUCTIONS OR INCREASES OF DOSAGE

You may need to increase the drug's dosage if your cat continues to appear anxious—his body is rigid or he cries constantly—or he resumes the deviant behavior. It's usually best to have your cat more relaxed than not, so if he sleeps much more than usual for a while but otherwise appears to be himself, the dosage is appropriate. If he's a total zombie and you fear his dosage is too high, be sure to seek counsel from your vet. An older cat is more likely to receive a lower dosage because of his slower metabolism.

SETBACK

If your cat experiences a setback (the deviant behavior returns), the dosage is usually increased until he can cope comfortably, and then it is subsequently slowly decreased to the maintenance dosage. Because the drug makes your cat feel more secure, he will usually recover and move ahead quickly after the setback.

The maintenance dosage may need to be increased during periods of extra stress—anything from a prolonged absence of a cat's person, continuous noise, a houseguest, or an illness in the family. The maintenance dosage should be increased for a short period covering the stressful situation, and reduced when the tension's over. It's usually best to wait and then reduce the dosage several days after circumstances are status quo because it takes time for the effects of the stress to diminish. Consult your cat's veterinarian.

DISCONTINUING THE DRUG

The drug can be stopped once the cat's catsonality changes enough so that he can interact and function without incident. The time frame will vary, depending on your cat's amount of anxiety, your support, and your cat's individual healing ability. When your cat's maintenance dosage is down to a very minute amount and he is snoozing frequently with a long period of no incidents, the drug can slowly be reduced and finally stopped. Be sure to consult your cat's veterinarian.

ADDICTION OR HARMFUL EFFECTS

There shouldn't be any deleterious effects if the drug is prescribed carefully and given sensibly, but it is best to have the vet evaluate your cat's blood chemistry first to determine if there are any problems the drug might aggravate or create.

The amount of medication can differ with each cat. It usually depends upon the cat's particular stress tolerance and how well his body absorbs the medication. He'll need a larger dosage if he's emotionally fragile and his absorption level is low. And if your cat has a bad reaction to one drug, another drug may be the solution.

You are in charge, and if you provide him with the support and confidence, eventually he can be weaned off his medication. If your cat is on medication for a long period, his veterinarian might want to recheck his blood chemistry and give him a general physical exam. Sometimes multiple drug trials may be needed to find the best drug.

It's important to remember that the drug is given *for auxiliary support*, and unless there is a behavioral program to change deviant habits and relieve anxiety, it's likely that your cat's symptoms will recur. Behavioral therapy is needed to provide a safe environment so new coping mechanisms can be integrated to produce a confident and self-assured cat. But if it's an *acute* problem rather than a *chronic* problem, the drug coupled with the caregiver's support can sometimes remedy the deviant behavior.

SKEPTICISM ABOUT DRUGS

If you have doubts and fears about sedating your cat, it might be best to find another way. Aside from prescription drugs, there are over-the-counter remedies, herbal calmers, and such homeopathic remedies as Bach flower essences and Boiron pellets. These alternatives should be used with proper direction and guidance.

There are also alternative health experts who can guide you. Magnet therapy is now being used as an alternative treatment, and there are specialists in this area.

CURE WITHOUT DRUGS

I have worked without the support of drug therapy with cats who have had extreme anxiety problems. But the cat's person needed to be extremely patient, because the recovery time was longer and the behavioral therapy sessions were extensive. Some of my techniques include behavioral modification recommendations and music therapy.

Ever since I have used music in my therapy with cats, I've relied less on drugs. (See Chapter 10.) The more relaxed a cat, the less apt he is to have an anxiety attack. When a cat can sustain feelings of trust and confidence, he becomes less vulnerable to stress and his deviant behavior subsides.

Effects of Your Anxiety

Your cat may be affected by your anxiety. He's quite an accurate barometer for just how anxious you are. If your cat feels neglected and is also picking up on your anxiety, he may start to meow, jump into your lap to soothe you, or misbehave.

Such reactions of your cat to your behavior are examples of fleeting anxiety and no cause for worry. But if you are frequently anxious without offering any comfort to your cat, his reactions may become more severe. A reflective and introverted cat, who tends to internalize his emotions, will probably manifest his reaction with a physical problem. A more verbal and extroverted cat might give a few hisses and cries throughout the day—perhaps a few nips—and may experience physical problems as well.

RECOVERY PERIOD

A recovery from a state of anxiety or stress varies with each patient, and there can be no exact prediction of a complete recovery date. A long-term problem would usually require extensive treatment. It takes time to reinforce new behavior patterns, so don't be alarmed if there are a few setbacks. As your cat's stress tolerance increases, his setbacks will decrease and finally disappear. Recovery should occur faster from then on.

RAGE

In some ways rage is a feeling that is similar to anxiety, but it is also a feeling that is unique unto itself. The usual signs are when your cat's ears flatten, his pupils dilate, his back ripples, his fur stands on end, and his tail jerks. An eerie, continuous yowl may accompany this. Anxiety can produce aggressive behavior, but rage is usually more dramatic and pronounced than anxiety. It erupts quickly, doesn't linger, and fades once the energy is expended, whereas anxiety—which is a state of apprehension and fear and/or worry—can prevail for a long time and sometimes indefinitely.

You can generally defuse rage by spritzing your cat with water from a plant mister or distracting him with a favorite game or toy. If the rage is directed at another cat, never get in the middle and risk the chance of becoming scratched or bitten. Don't try to pick up a fighting cat! Use the above methods to separate the cats. Once you have removed the source of rage, be prepared to make yourself scarce if your cat continues to be cranky. He may need to be alone to recover from his rage.

SADNESS

Your cat's eyes may take on a sad expression, his spirits may decline, and he may generally deviate from his routine behavior to communicate his woefulness. If it's a physical problem that has made him uncomfortable and sad, he may try to draw attention to the source of his discomfort. Such a physical problem makes your cat unhappy because he feels awful. If his stress target (the most vulnerable part of his body) is affected, such as his bladder or rectum, he may avoid the litter box to communicate his distress.

On the other hand, sadness over a change in his daily life—such as the loss of a companion or friend, a feeling of neglect, or culture shock—can trigger a medical problem.

The more aware you are of your cat's feelings, the easier it will be for you to interpret his actions. This can only pave the way for a happier and healthier relationship. You might like to refer to the chart I've created to help you to identify your cat's emotions.

HOW TO RECOGNIZE YOUR CAT'S EMOTIONS

Emotion	Stimulus	Cat's Response
Happiness	Stroking, cuddling, eating, nursing, close contact, snoozing, being alone with person or companion	Face and body relax; there may be a smile on the face; purring, stretching, kneading, licking

Emotion	Stimulus	Cat's Response
Controlled happiness	Qualified contact: cat may purr as he sits in your lap but object when you try to touch him	All of above, but if his tail flicks or his body ripples it's his signal that he wants whatever the stimulus is to stop
Sadness	Sickness, loss of companion or person, feeling of neglect, separation anxiety	Lethargy, dull coat, loss of appetite, bizarre toilet habits, scratching or pawing at various parts of the skin, reclusiveness
Rage	Presence of new or alien animal or person, accident, cat spat, tomcat or unspayed syndrome	Body contracts; rapid breathing; flattened ears, puffy tail, flicking tail, arched back, loud yowl. Cat may attack person or animal who was the source of his anxiety or may displace his aggression to an innocent victim. Rage erupts quickly
Fleeting or expectation anxiety	Short-term stimulus (example: fly on the loose that cat wants to catch)	Flexes body muscles; makes chutter-chutter noise
Prolonged anxiety	Lingering presence of alien person or animal; tomcat or unspayed syndrome; presence of sick animal whether obviously ill or not	All of above may occur, or a few of the above responses and medical problems may be triggered
Overstimulation anxiety	Becomes too aroused from being petted or held; can't handle energy charge	Tail flicks, ears flatten, body ripples; may bite or scratch if action continues

Emotion	Stimulus	Cat's Response
Separation anxiety	Temporarily or permanently separated from person or companion	May cause cat to become insecure, trigger anxiety and take it out on companion or person; may also trigger medical problems
Eager anticipation	Something that a cat wants from you (example: to sit in your lap, have head scratched, have you change his litter box)	Stare at you, meow, jump up beside you, rub head against your hand, circle litter box, run back and forth to it
Dread anticipation	Your cat knows what's going to happen next and doesn't like it (example: grooming, traveling, ear cleaning)	Disappears, body ripples, tail flicks; may try to pretend he's napping to delay action
Ambivalent anticipation	Your cat wants and doesn't want something (example: wants to join party but too shy)	Encourages petting but runs off quickly because can't accept high energy and has to discharge it

YOUR EMOTIONS AND YOUR CAT

The first time you realized how much your cat was affected by your moods you were stunned. After all, you didn't change your behavior toward him and you still loved him more than ever. But you had just returned from a meeting with someone who really upset you. Your cat met you at the door, but instead of hanging out with you, he disappeared under the bed. You didn't see him again until after your bath. He was still a bit tentative but finally curled up beside you on your bed. How could he be so sensitive, you wondered, and how did he get his first clue of how you felt? You're still mystified about his uncanny reactions to your behavior. He seems to mirror your moods.

How Your Cat Senses Your Feelings

A cat is very sensitive to sounds and body language, because these are his primary means of communication. When you are relaxed and happy, your body expands and your movements flow. It's difficult for your body to be expansive when your thoughts are not happy and your spirit is awry. Your mind, spirit, and body are connected. They do not act independently. It's this connection that your cat is sensitive to, and his behavior will very likely *mirror your feelings.* This ability makes your cat exquisitely in tune with your feelings and rarely enables you to outwit him.

Your Cat's Reaction to Your Moods

Your cat is attracted to you when you are mellow, pensive, or even depressed because your energy is nonthreatening. Your body relaxes, and your cat is drawn to the low-key energy. He may very likely cuddle next to you. Why not? Your energy soothes him.

When you are angry, hysterically sad, or happy, your cat will probably retreat or hide. He's repelled by your body and verbal tension. Whereas if you were crying softly, he would be likely to sit beside you. It's not unusual for your cat to want to hang out with you when you're sick and bedridden. He's attracted to your relaxed, languid energy—perfect for his meditation time. He fills the role of a full-time nurse.

Your cat will probably distance himself from you when you're overenergetic or manic. At this time he can't or doesn't want to deal with your jangled energy. It makes him uncomfortable. Loud laughing may also agitate your cat. If your laughing is directed at him, he may even become withdrawn and not appear until he's forgiven you. Dignity is a cat's strong suit.

Your cat may react to your anxiety or stress by becoming ill or aggravating an already existing health problem. This can happen to your cat if he is especially sensitive. A senior cat is usually more vulnerable to your mood swings and changes in lifestyle.

Your cat may also choose to be near you when you're eating—especially if it's something you adore. He's seduced by your contented energy and wants to bask in it.

Your cat is a born medium for fluctuations in surrounding energy fields—both human and animal. This endows him with the gift I refer to as cat sense. He's able to sense actions through a shift in energy sometimes before it actually happens. He doesn't even have to "see" it to get the message.

A prime example of this is when you've quietly stretched out on the rug with your favorite novel in hand and your cat appears from the far end of your house, greets you with a stretch, and plops down on your chest. He was attracted to your comfortable, quiet energy and wanted to be part of it.

The antithesis of this is, for example, when you were unable to balance your checkbook and felt like you wanted to scream, or at the very least to moan. Suddenly your cat appears and starts to scream at you. This is his way of telling you that you should calm down, take a deep breath, and not disturb him.

Yes, your cat is an accurate barometer of your feelings. He may not be an intellectual whiz kid, but his emotional intelligence is great. Combined with his gift of cat sense, his emotional smarts allow him to frustrate any of your efforts to deceive him.

Catsonalities and Catcentricities

You can still see your first cat as he sat perched at the top of his cat tree with a look of supremacy and self-love. He had an air of confidence that always made you smile. But you had two cats at the time. Your other cat was reserved and somewhat passive. He let the other cat take the lead. You often wondered what contributed to your first cat's catsonality. What was it that made him such a top cat in almost every way?

TOP CAT SUPREME

Actions that define a top cat supreme:

1. He is fascinated by people and affectionate toward them
2. He reacts immediately to frustrating situations, externalizing his energy

3. He is bold and friendly

4. He leads the way in investigating new things you bring into the house, running over to sniff and climb around them

5. He is the first to check out changes outside

You may have a cat who assumes top-cat position but who is frequently overaggressive with his companion cats or with people. He probably was not blessed with all the ingredients that make a top cat, but instead is dominant and aggressive out of fear and insecurity—he's a top cat, but not a top cat supreme. It's not uncommon for him to misbehave when he feels especially threatened. You can ease his insecurity by making him feel important and in control.

Ingredients for top cat supreme:

1. Parents who were robust and emotionally thick-skinned

2. An unremarkable or normal gestation period and birth

3. The pick of the mother cat's nipples and nursed for ten weeks

4. Few littermates who were content to let him or her be the ringleader

5. A clean bill of health by the veterinarian

6. A nurturing human

7. Adequate diet and exercise

8. Congenial companion cat

ZEN CAT

A Zen cat has the tranquility and grace of a woodland pool. His demeanor attracts love and acceptance. The following factors may contribute to his easygoing catsonality.

Ingredients for a Zen cat:

1. Birth without incident or trauma
2. Healthy mother and father
3. A mother cat who fed and cared for her litter
4. Adoption at younger than ten weeks old but later abandonment
5. A constitution hardy enough to cope with the rigors of life on the street or the stress of living in an animal shelter

Actions that define a Zen cat:

1. This cat has seen it all and is unfazed by noisy appliances, new people, etc. He sometimes even ignores their presence.
2. He calms his companion cats when they are upset, coming over to give them a loving wash.

TIMID CAT

You adore this cat, but he acts so frightened. Your friends refer to him as the phantom cat. However, now and again he deigns to make an appearance for company—if he gets the feeling they're going to be around for a while. You adopted him when he was around nine weeks old from the family that owned his mother, and he was timid right from the start. Friends of yours adopted his littermates, and none of them are timid. What happened to him?

Ingredients for a timid cat:

1. He was the last of the litter to be born or he was the runt.

2. He never got the choicest nipple, often being pushed aside by his littermates.

3. His lack of resemblance to his mother led her to favor the kittens who looked more like her.

4. His mother cat nursed her kittens for only about five weeks, and then lost interest in her kittens.

5. He was always shy with his people and kept his distance, though he played with his littermates.

Actions that define a timid cat:

1. He's always on guard, even when he's curled up in your lap.

2. When visitors stop by or at any sudden loud noise outside or in, he hides under the bed or sofa.

3. He's afraid of household appliances like the vacuum cleaner and the blender.

You've certainly tried to make him feel loved, and he has become a bit less reserved, but his rocky start paved the way for his timidity. He does not possess the emotional thick skin or constitution that allows him to roll with the punches. Yes, he has low self-esteem that was formed when he was in his mother's womb. Continue to nurture him with patience and understanding. As he grows in years, he'll gain in confidence. Time is the key unless you create a special program for him or perhaps engage professional help.

ALOOF CAT

This cat loves to play, hangs out with you, sleeps at the foot of your bed, and purrs when you pet him. But he squirms and runs when you try to hold him. Once, when he was really tired, he let you cuddle him briefly, but then he snapped at you and bolted. The following factors contributed to your cat's aloofness.

Ingredients for an aloof cat:

1. He probably did not have prolonged intimacy with his mother or littermates, or when he did, he wasn't fulfilled. That is why, when he becomes aroused or overstimulated, he becomes doubtful. He either flees or fights.

2. As long as he feels free to move as he pleases, he's not threatened. But when he is confined or held, he becomes overwhelmed by a surge of unresolved anxiety from his kittenhood, and he flees from the source of his present anxiety.

3. When you try to become intimate with him, he feels confined and becomes fearful, which prevents any sustained intimacy.

CATCENTRICITIES

Interaction with Other Cats

A cat can play medical detective. Although it may seem unusual, it's not uncommon for a cat to suddenly avoid and reject a feline companion with whom he's been fast friends. Such behavior is often precipitated by an illness in the companion that the healthy cat sensed. It caused him to be anxious, and he rejected his sick companion because of his discomfort. His feline diagnosis may have kicked in even before his sick companion displayed any clinical signs. After a visit to the vet, it became apparent why there was a chink in the relationship.

Other cats may nurse their sick companions. This type of cat may even nurse his invalid companion until the end. But not every cat has the feline nurse instinct that allows him to cope with a sick companion's discomfort without becoming disturbed and tense. A Florence Nightincat is indeed a treasure.

Uncanny Rituals

Chosen objects: It never ceases to amaze you that your cat will crawl into the smallest basket for his nap or plop himself on what appears to be the most likely object. Your cat has probably chosen the basket because a similar basket pleased him when he was a kitten, and he enjoys both the familiarity and your affectionate reaction. His fondness for unlikely objects may also develop because of their particular texture or his association of them with good feelings.

Eating: Another of your cat's rituals is to work for your acceptance or company while he eats. He meows and runs to his food dish and continues to mew until you appear beside him. Sometimes he'll be content with a few strokes and praise while he starts to eat. But other times he demands your company longer. It's almost as if he needs your approval to fully enjoy his food. His need for your company and approval may be because he didn't have enough attention and nourishment from his mother cat, so you've become his surrogate mother or security object that he associates with food. Your presence provides him with the comfort and companionship he lacked as a kitten.

Toilet time: What really amuses you is that your cat chooses to use his litter box when you use the toilet. Or else one of his favorite routines is to sit in your lap while you sit on the toilet seat. His entire body relaxes and he purrs nonstop.

This behavior occurs because your body becomes relaxed when you use the toilet and he wants to share in your relaxation. What could be more intimate than to be a lap cat at such a time? What's more—you're captive and he doesn't have to share your attention. He's free from interference.

The right spot: Another ritual occurs when he decides to stretch out on the floor, bed, or wherever. First he circles the designated area a few times and gives it a few glances before he finally takes possession. Sometimes he may even knead it with his paws.

Dress-up time: Something else that pleases your cat, which is quite uncatlike, is that he purrs and relaxes when you put a bandanna or ribbon around his neck. His pleased reaction is because you probably tell him how handsome he looks, and he reacts to your praise. This is a fine example of mutual admiration, and it is great for your cat's self-esteem.

Visitors: You are fascinated by your cat's reactions to your friends. Sometimes he avoids those who are enthusiastic cat lovers and instead seeks out those who are indifferent, fearful, or allergic. He may not always be in the mood for a display of high-energy affection from a cat devotee. However, he may be attracted to the indifferent person because of the challenge and because this person places no demands on him. Your fearful or allergic friend may intrigue him, or he may be bothered by their angst and approach them in an attempt to stamp it out. Perhaps in this case opposites clearly attract!

Energy barometer: Sometimes he has the strangest reactions to your behavior. The other day you were on the telephone in the midst of a real estate discussion and he came over to be stroked. As you chatted, you stroked his back and he stretched out on the sofa beside you. Suddenly he lightly nipped your fingers. You stopped stroking him. He'd made his point. He continued to hang out beside you and soon dozed off. This incident really baffled you.

Although your cat initially wanted to be stroked, he wanted only so much. Your high energy and intensity on the phone probably overstimulated him. He decided that he was more comfortable beside you without contact. His reaction was a definitive statement as to your level of energy and tension.

Yes, your cat's quirky or wacky behavior is usually triggered by a particular need. So when he appears weird or out of line, stop and think why he might react in such a manner. You might discover something new about your own behavior.

Over the Edge

One minute he's your best friend, full of purrs and curled next to your arm. Suddenly he pulls himself up, nips your arm, and dashes away. Another time he's nestled beside you on the bed and with no apparent provocation he lets out a few hisses, scratches your leg, and tears out of the bedroom. This abusive behavior is also showered on his companion cat. When he's loving he's a dream cat, but his flip side is dreadful. How can such a lover boy be such a terror?

Ingredients for an attack cat:

1. Poor lover boy just has no control over his temper. He can't sustain his serenity and lashes out when he feels out of control. It doesn't take much for him to feel this way.

2. He's one more example of a cat who didn't get his share of the nurturing that he needed from the mom cat (see Chapter 9).

3. Although he appears to be a tough cookie, inside he's quite vulnerable.

4. He's easily startled and/or frustrated. When this occurs, he attacks the source of his anxiety.

There is hope for him to modify this surly streak, and the right agenda can keep him from going over the edge. Nip his aggressive behavior in the bud by distracting him. If his back ripples, tail flicks, or he starts to glare, throw a toy or object with gusto so his energy becomes absorbed in the activity. Announce your transitions so he isn't taken by surprise.

Don't expect any two cats to be exactly the same—even if they're littermates with the same parents—because catsonality depends on the individual cat's total makeup or constitution. Moreover, even when you know your cat's catsonality type, don't expect to understand your cat all the time, because now and again he'll throw you a curve. That's exactly why a cat's catsonality is so endearing.

Professional Services

You try to be selective about the professionals you choose for *your* personal services, and you feel that it's most important that you do the same for your cat. It's especially important because your cat is dependent upon your choices. His well-being is in your hands.

Your cat's life is precious, and that's why you want to make sure he's healthy and you're in touch with all you can do to prevent problems before they occur. That's why you must have a competent and caring veterinarian who can treat your cat when he's ill and also make you aware of how you can contribute to your cat's good health. However, you're not quite sure how to choose the best veterinarian for your cat.

CHOOSING A VETERINARIAN

Solicit recommendations from your friends and acquaintances and check your local yellow pages for vets in your neighborhood. However, don't settle on a vet for convenience's sake if there's someone better whose office is farther away. You might even phone your local veterinary medical association for names of new veterinarians who have recently opened offices in your area.

Make a list of possible vets and phone their offices. A receptionist's phone manner is usually a reflection of the hospital. It should be courteous, patient, friendly, and informative. Ask if twenty-four-hour medical care is available to handle emergencies (many hospitals offer this important service). Make sure that specialists are consulted and used when the occasion arises. Ask for a current fee schedule. If possible, speak to the vet to help form your impression.

Visit the hospitals that interest you to check out their environment. Be aware of cleanliness, odors, and light and noise. The staff should be kind, helpful, and alert. Notice if you and other clients get a comfortable feeling from the waiting room.

Ask to have a tour of the hospital. If you can, check the areas where the animals are hospitalized to be certain they are clean, well-kept, and not crowded. There should be a separate section for infectious patients. If there are boarders, they should be kept in a separate area. Cats should have individual litter boxes, and dogs should be walked often. Plants and other homey touches are a boost to the general environment. The care and appearance of hospital adoptees and residents is a direct reflection of the hospital.

Speak to the vet and be conscious of the vet's manner. He or she should be talking to you and not *at* you. Try to sense if the vet really likes cats. Your impression of his or her associates should be favorable so you can be confident that good medicine and patient care are trademarks of the hospital. Ask if house calls are available when imperative.

Visiting privileges should be available for hospitalized patients, and special dietary requests should be considered.

The hospital should treat euthanasia, cremation, and burial in a respectful manner. Grief counseling is a plus if the hospital offers such a service or makes referrals.

When you've made your choice and taken your cat in for his first appointment, be very aware of the vet's cat-side manner. It should be compassionate and firm, but gentle and thorough. Your cat should be cared for like a patient, not an object, and you should be treated as a person. Your questions and feelings should be considered and respected. The vet's assistant should also handle your cat with care.

Your bill should be clearly itemized and your questions should be answered courteously and satisfactorily.

If, after the appointment, your cat does not appear to be stressed, you feel confident about the vet, and follow-up on phone calls and other communication are complete and prompt, you've found the best person. But if not, you have the freedom to make another choice. All medical records are your property and can be transferred to another vet upon your request.

Because your cat cannot tell you what ails him, his medical care must be put in the hands of a sensitive and capable individual whose ability and judgment you can trust. If you're uneasy about the veterinarian, your anxious feelings will be communicated through your body language and increase your cat's discomfort and stress. You must have peace of mind about your cat's welfare. Choosing the right veterinarian will provide emotional as well as medical benefits. You owe it to yourself and your cat to select the right veterinarian.

CAT THERAPISTS AND BEHAVIORISTS

When your cat has a behavioral problem, you can usually sort it out yourself or with the help of your friends. But

there may come a time when you need an expert to trou-
bleshoot your cat's behavioral quirk. Don't let deviant behavior continue for too long. The sooner you begin to
modify his behavior, the easier it will be. A cat is indeed
a creature of habit and prefers not to change his routine
unless he's decided it's time for a change.

Your veterinarian may be able to recommend an expert
to help you, or may even have such a person available to
come to the office for consultations. Some therapists do
behavioral consultations by telephone. I am associated with
two hospitals, where I do consultations and am also available for telephone and mail consultations. But I find that,
if the problem is a chronic one or one that is wreaking
great havoc with cat and person, a house call usually works
best. It gives me the opportunity to see the cat's environment, to defuse some of the tension by my presence, and
to use my technique of music therapy to relax both cat and
person (see Chapter 10).

How to Choose the Best Therapist or Behaviorist

Recommendations from friends, veterinarians, books,
cat magazines, or radio or TV should lead you to the
best person.

Try to talk to the person so you can decide if his or
her approach will work for you. This is a helpful way to
see if the therapist or behaviorist is on your wavelength. If
you're very analytical, you might prefer the person to use
more of a behavioristic than a humanistic approach, em-
phasizing techniques for modifying your cat's behavior
rather than delving into emotions and your cat's reaction
to your behavior. You may also want to ask for names of
clients you can call for references.

I am available for house calls and phone consultations
nationally and internationally. Also, I see appointments

with or without cats at Westside Veterinary Center (220 West 83 Street, New York, NY 10024, 212-580-1800) and The Animal Clinic of New York (1623 First Avenue, New York, NY 10028, 212-628-5580). For general information, I can be reached at 212-741-0397 or www.the-cat-therapist.com. I also work extensively on cases with many veterinary hospitals.

Don't hesitate to ask about the fee and the time allowed for each appointment. During the first appointment you'll be able to get an idea if the person has the same feeling you do about cats. It's important to have someone who's sympathetic to your relationship with your cat.

If your cat has a stressful reaction to the person you choose, you might want to consider another expert. But don't expect your cat's problems to disappear immediately. Sometimes one consultation or session can alter your cat's deviant behavior. But frequently a cat will need more help. Finally, it would be great preventative medicine if each cat had an annual behavioral checkup to keep him on the right path and to nip a problem in the bud.

CAT SITTERS

You'd love to take your cat away with you, but for many reasons that just won't work. You don't have anyone to live in while you're away, your cat doesn't like to leave home, and there isn't a neighbor who can tend to your cat. What should you do?

There are professional cat sitters you can engage to help fill the void and ease the separation anxiety. Even if you are away only for a night, it's vital to your cat's health to have someone stop in. Check with your veterinarian, your friends, and local pet supply shops for available candidates and make certain to ask for references to confirm reliability. There is also a national cat sitter's association that can be consulted. (They should have a toll-free number and may be on line.)

Tips for selecting the appropriate cat sitter:

1. Invite the person to come over so you can judge your cat's reaction. Even if your cat is shy with most visitors, you can still get some indication of the person's demeanor. A person who forces himself or herself on your cat should be avoided.

2. Explain and show the person your cat's daily regimen.

3. If possible, try to select a person who lives in your neighborhood.

4. Ask if the person has a substitute in case of an emergency. You should have available the name of a nearby person who has your keys and can arrange for another cat sitter for double security.

Instructions for the cat sitter:

1. List your cat's food and number of feedings (remember to leave an ample supply of food, extra dishes in case of breakage, and cat litter).

2. Ask him or her not to open your windows (unless they have full screens).

3. Request that any electrical appliances are turned off when the sitter leaves.

4. Inform your cat sitter that he or she should check to see that the stove is off after each visit.

5. Let the cat sitter know that he or she should be aware of cat's whereabouts to make certain your cat isn't locked in a closet or somewhere when the sitter leaves.

6. Ask the sitter to leave the radio on with soft music to keep your cat company. Most cats appreciate this.

7. Write down your phone numbers and itinerary and your date of return.

8. Leave the number and address of your cat's veterinarian.

9. Make sure the sitter practices locking and unlocking your door before you leave.

10. If your cat needs medication, write down the amount and frequency of dosage. (You should also give the person a demonstration of how to administer such medication beforehand.)

11. Specify location of your cat's carrier in case of an emergency.

12. If the cat sitter is to live in while you're away, make certain to write down any particularly quirky habits of your cat.

13. Fasten a sign to your front door that indicates there's a cat in residence to be rescued in the event of fire or other disaster.

You also might want to leave a notebook for your cat sitter to record your cat's behavior while you're away.

Before you leave for your trip, give your cat a hug and repeat a few times that you'll be back soon. If your cat is comfortable with the sound of voices on your answering machine, you can call and leave him messages while you're away. However, if hearing phone messages agitates him, make sure to turn the volume down. When you return home, your cat's spirits and state of his comforts will let you know if the cat sitter should return.

GROOMERS

If you're not a conscientious groomer and you have a long-haired cat, you'll have to make arrangements to have your cat groomed by a professional. Your veterinarian may offer this service, and you may also be able to find groomers who work out of their own offices or ones who are willing to come to your home so your cat doesn't have to travel.

Check with your cat-caring friends for recommendations or consult the yellow pages. Pet supply shops and your veterinarian may also have suggestions. It's important that you check references, so you have an idea of the potential groomer's way with cats. Try to arrange an interview with each person you're interested in so you and your cats are not in for a total surprise. If your cats have a gender preference, respect their wishes. Remember, if the groomer you select doesn't pass their inspection, go on to the next.

PET FINDERS

Let us hope your cat never goes astray. But if so, there is an organization named Pet Finders that you can engage to help you find him. They can be reached at an 800 number where you can register your cat's vital information. They will provide you with the various lists of lost cats from shelters and private individuals.

A microchip can be placed in your cat's ear, or a tattoo can be made on the ear. These include his identification and can be accessed by a veterinary hospital or shelter if your cat becomes lost. Your cat's veterinarian should be able to supply you with the contacts for this procedure.

There are also organizations such as 1-800-Help-4-Pets, that furnish a twenty-four-hour national pet help line. They supply you with identification tags that are engraved with a toll-free telephone number and your cat's personal identification number. The tag connects the finder of your cat with trained personnel. You can call their number for costs and other information.

BURIAL AND MEMORIAL SERVICES

When your cat's end has come, the following information should be helpful. There are special animal cemeteries and companies that provide well-built burial chests if you choose to bury your beloved cat. Custom-engraved wooden memorials and marble ones are also available. There are also funeral parlors for animals. Magazines, such as *Cat Fancy* and *Cats*, contain numerous listings for these services (see also Chapter 16 for additional information).

Cremation

If you choose to have your cat cremated, your cat's veterinarian can usually arrange to have the crematory service pick up your cat's body at the hospital or at your home. The ashes are returned in a container if you request them.

GRIEF THERAPY FOR YOU

The loss of a beloved cat can be very painful. To help with mourning, the services of a bereavement counselor may be invaluable. There are counselors who work with groups that meet frequently or offer private appointments. Arrange to speak with the counselor before you schedule a session. Sometimes it is possible to arrange such a session at your veterinarian's office.

I offer such services to help people with their bereavement and also treat their late cat's companion, who are often greatly affected by the demise of their buddy—even if the relationship was not an amicable one.

You can usually locate a bereavement counselor through your veterinarian, word of mouth, or your telephone book. There are support groups and counselors who see clients privately. Don't deny yourself this peace of mind that is so vital at such a grievous time.

Animal communicators, spiritual healers, and psychics offer alternative ways to understand your cat. You obtain referrals through your veterinarian, friends, or classified ads. But be sure to get references before you engage their services.

As cat lovers become more sophisticated in their cat care, more and more professional services are created. You can afford to be particular. There isn't a monopoly!

"Heel, fetch, beg—that's a life?"

Companionship

Your cat is only sixteen months old, and he is really wired. If there were a Cat Olympics, he'd be a gold medalist. He used to have play dates in the hall with the kitten who lived next door. The kitten was a black female and he really adored her. But the kitten moved away. You tried play dates with a couple of grown cats, but your guy really loved this kitten. He often has a frustrated look when he's bouncing off the walls and you won't play with him. You're not too keen on a second cat, but you want your guy to be happy and well adjusted, so you do decide to get a second cat. But one of your friends brought home a kitten for her cat and it was a disaster. You think that there must be a painless way to introduce a new kitten.

Yes, there is a method of introduction that I have devised that is painless and successful. You'll find it works quickly and easily.

CHOOSING A KITTEN FOR YOUR CAT

Matching Catsonality Types

This list of catsonality types should help you to select your cat's appropriate kitten.

- Marilyn Monroe type: If your cat is beautiful to look at—a real glamour puss—choose a kitten who can hold a candle to her looks but won't outdo her.

- Mother Teresa type: If your cat loves to nurture and protect, a timid kitten would suit him perfectly.

- Glenn Close type: If your cat is an elegant grande dame or gent, avoid an especially lively kitten. A low-energy kitten would be best for your cat.

- Michael Jordan type: If your cat is an athlete—gold medal material—a live-wire kitten would be an ideal match.

- Clint Eastwood: If your cat is altruistic and bold in a low-key manner you can have your pick of kittens.

- Ralph Fiennes type: If your cat is dashing but understated, a mellow but striking kitten would suit.

- Subtle innate beauty: If your cat is one whose beauty is from within and is not the type to win any beauty pageants, don't select a kitten who is drop-dead gorgeous. Why gamble with your cat's self-esteem?

- Cat-oriented kitten/Greta Garbo type: If your cat has always been somewhat introverted and shy with people, choose a cat-oriented kitten who interacts happily with his littermates and other cats. Your cat needs a kitten that prefers felines to people; he needs a kitten that will strike up a relationship with him. Eventually, the new kitten will make overtures to you. This type of kitten will make it that much easier for you to keep a low profile, which will hasten your cat's acceptance.

• Feral kitten/Sean Penn type: If your cat tends to be possessive of you and even a bit aggressive when agitated, a somewhat feral kitten that has had some contact with people is the best bet for your cat. This kitten will be less than interested in you, but he will be totally interested in your cat. By the time he becomes socialized, your cat will be his mentor and love. Don't get a feral kitten if you don't think you'll have the patience to wait for the kitten's acceptance of you.

• Multi-oriented kitten/Tom Hanks type: Your cat is an equal opportunity type. He loves everybody with few exceptions—when a dog came to visit, he sat beside the dog and wanted to lick his tail; a foray into the hall brought him face-to-face with a neighbor's cat, and he rolled over to show his tummy— his best match is a kitten that is cat-friendly, people friendly, superplayful and feckless. You want a kitten to match your cat's versatility and abundant energy.

• Mellow kitten/Meryl Streep type: If your cat is a dream who never does anything to irk you and is quiet and conservative in his behavior, choose a kitten who is of similar nature but with a bit of playfulness. This type of kitten should motivate your cat to greater and grander action.

Choice of Color

A cat is color sensitive. Different colors may have distinctive scents; various color patterns may have a singularity that affects your cat. For example, one day your cat encountered a neighbor's gray cat in the hall, and it was nearly a disaster. When you lived in the suburbs, he used to adore a black cat that came to visit.

If your cat has had an aversion to cats of a specific color, try to avoid that color and select a color that is neutral or a color that you know he prefers. His own color is familiar and nonthreatening. A mother cat will often prefer her kittens who look like her to the ones who differ. Familiarity breeds friendship.

WILBOURN WAY OF INTRODUCING A KITTEN TO YOUR CAT

Many a cat has met a new kitten or cat with no special ceremony and it has been fine. But to avoid any major catastrophe, I have found my method of introduction to be painless and successful.

Prearrival Preparations

- Don't schedule the introduction on a day of a gala party or when you're expecting visitors or renovating your home.
- Try to bring the new kitten home in the morning or early afternoon.
- Kitten-proof your home: put away your favorite ornaments and seal any holes in the wall or floor that a kitten might nestle in.
- Provide separate food and water dishes for the kitten. An additional litter box is optional.

The Kitten's Escort

Arrange for someone to bring the new kitten to your home. Select a person your cat hasn't befriended. This will prevent your cat from forming a negative association; he will feel that you and your other friends are not responsible for the newcomer's arrival. You can't assume that if *you* present the kitten as a gift your cat will accept it. *Remember,* a cat prefers to call the shots. Let the kitten be his find.

The escort is needed for only a brief appearance—to escort the newcomer in but not to linger.

The Kitten's Arrival

- Start the day with his favorite breakfast.

- Praise and hug your cat.

- Don't tell him you have a surprise for him. Let the kitten be *his* surprise. But remind him that he's the best boy!

- Either leave the front door ajar for the escort to let himself or herself in or give him or her your house keys.

- Take your cat with you into the bedroom with your cat's favorite things and perhaps a new toy. Keep the door closed.

- Have the escort deposit the new kitten in the cat carrier in the bathroom, with litter box nearby. The escort should open the carrier.

- Have the escort leave the kitten in the bathroom, with the door slightly ajar, and leave your home.

- Open the bedroom door after you hear the outer door close. Your cat will *eventually* slip out and discover *his new friend.*

- Once the door is opened, say good-bye to your cat and leave the bedroom! Don't dillydally. Head straight for the door and *don't* try to spot the kitten. Your cat is in charge.

- An afternoon of entertainment or projects for you alone should be on your agenda for at least five hours.
- Trust your cat to take care of himself and his kitten.

Home Again

When you return home, remember that the kitten is invisible to you. You should pay zero attention to him. But if and when you must interact with the kitten, mention your other cat's name in the process so he'll feel in charge and connected. You might say: "Brady, I have to clean your cat's ears, give him a pill, etc., on your behalf." Brady won't get the literal meaning, but he'll sense that your interaction with his kitten is in his interest. This easy technique will prevent rivalry. Even after they've bonded, mention your cat's name when you interact with his kitten. You can also refer to the kitten as, for example, Brady's Blackie.

Clandestine Affection

Your cat won't be deceived if you sneak attention to the kitten on the sly. He can't be deceived because a cat is extremely sensitive to fluctuations in energy. He doesn't have to "see" because he can feel or sense what is happening. Why risk the upset? The kitten will not lack affection because your cat will be the provider.

Visitors

Your friends should follow the same hands-off policy with your cat's kitten. Don't invite over any company that can't concentrate on your cat while the two bond. If such people can't be avoided, let your guys hang out in another room.

Bedtime Privileges

The kitten should not be allowed on your bed even if your cat has never slept with you. He would be deeply offended if his kitten did. But if your cat sleeps with you and tolerates his kitten in bed, terrific! If necessary, you can sequester the kitten at bedtime. But if this agitates your cat, sequester yourself in the bedroom.

Time Element

I have encountered some cats who have bonded with their kitten on the first day. Others have been more wary. A relationship takes time to flower. The more relaxed you are, the easier it will be for their relationship to grow. If your cat withdraws or disappears, seek him out. He needs you! He may feel that you favor his kitten. Their relationship will suffer if you try to bond with his kitten before he does. The more you are away from home, the quicker they'll connect. You might even plan a short holiday and give the cat sitter the same instructions you have been following.

Jealousy

If it appears that three are a crowd and you feel neglected by your cat, don't panic because you'll soon have the two of them purring on your lap. Remind yourself that the tighter they become with each other, the happier and healthier you'll all be. Your cat's source of companionship and entertainment (if he's an indoor cat) is limited. You can seek outside stimuli when you wish, but he's stuck with you for better or worse.

Your Rule of Thumb

Repeat to yourself that the kitten is for your cat. It's important for your cat to bond with the kitten before you do. After they've visibly bonded, wait about ten days before you interact with the kitten. Telltale signs of acceptance are if they groom each other, play together, and nestle. The more they repeat this intimate behavior, the tighter they'll become, which is why you don't want to be hasty in forming your relationship with your cat's kitten.

Your cat has had 100 percent of your attention until now, and you don't want him to feel that the kitten will deprive him of you. That's why it's best to be cautious. The slightest gesture might make your cat jealous. So that's why the hands-off-kitten policy works until they're an obvious "item."

Paramount Reminders

Wait ten days from the day that the two visibly bond before you interact with the kitten. If you jump in sooner, your cat may resent the kitten and keep his distance. Patience will pay great dividends. Even if the kitten crawls into your lap, be brave and gently but emphatically remove the kitten. Don't jeopardize your cat's trust. Your temporary rejection of the kitten will not produce permanent scars. The kitten has your cat to rely on—even if it takes a bit of perseverance and convincing on the kitten's part. Remember the kitten is invisible to you (with necessary or practical exceptions). Be brave! You are not cruel and your "hands off" policy should produce a terrific feline friendship.

CHOOSING A CAT FOR YOUR KITTEN

You already have a kitten, but you've decided that a full-grown cat would be a great teacher and companion.

Review the catsonality-type pointers on pages 109–110, so, if possible, you don't start off with incompatible catsonalities. You don't want to adopt a sedate, introverted cat for a bouncing kitten. Follow the Wilbourn way of introducing a new cat to your home, but because a cat is usually less adaptable than a kitten, you can immediately be quite friendly with the new cat. The kitten will follow your lead. Give your kitten a little less attention so he'll definitely seek the new cat out. Remember to mention the cat's name whenever you interact with your kitten, so the cat will feel included and in control. As in the introduction of a kitten to a cat, the more you're away from home, the quicker the two will bond. It shouldn't take long for your kitten to win the new cat over. But don't force them on each other. The kitten will probably be relentless in his quest to befriend the new cat. Although an intact, sickly cat may not bond well with you or your kitten, if you've adopted a spayed or neutered healthy cat, you should soon have a friendly duo.

CHOOSING A CAT FOR YOUR CAT

You don't want to adopt a kitten for your cat, and you've decided that your cat's new companion should be at least two years old. You're aware that a senior cat might be inflexible and too sedate for your cat. Again, use my pointers for matching catsonalities.

Make the Introduction

Arrange to have a neutral party bring the newcomer in. However, the newcomer should be kept in a separate room with all of his creature comforts. Place a screen door on the entrance to the room where the newcomer is to be kept so the two cats can view each other without physical contact. If a screen door isn't possible, you can use a piece of Plexiglas or half screens that are expandable and stack from floor to top of door frame. Fasten to the door frame with Velcro. You can later place the newcomer's food in view of the doorway to persuade him to venture forth.

Within a couple of days you can try to engage the cats' interest with toy or string dangled in front of the doorway or screen. Plan to spend most of the day away from home. After your return, whenever you enter the new cat's domain, tell your cat you're checking up on the newcomer so he doesn't have to do it. Tend to the newcomer's needs but don't be overaffectionate because your cat will sense it—even if the door is closed. Mention your cat's name in conversation with the newcomer so your cat will feel included.

Grand Entrance

When you notice that the two cats don't hiss and scream at each other and are perhaps even curious about each other without malice, you can open the door or remove the bottom screen so they can venture to and fro. But don't sit and stare at them. Arrange to bring them together at a time when you and both cats are relaxed.

If there is a major spat, separate the two by spritzing them with water from a plant mister. Repeat this process the next day and try to escort the newcomer back to his room before there is an upset. As their relationship improves, you can increase their time together. They'll probably do best when you're away from home, because your doubts and worry can influence their behavior. Above all, don't try to rush the process. You want their relationship to have a firm foundation. Repetition with reduction of threat is what they need to build this relationship.

Top Cat Role

It may turn out that the newcomer becomes the leader, the top cat—especially if the newcomer is a mover and a shaker and if your first cat tends to be laid-back and cautious. Such a situation would perhaps give your cat a role model who teaches him to be more friendly and aggressive.

Curtail Rivalry

Whenever you interact with one cat, refer to the other by name, so you don't make either cat feel excluded. A simple example is: "Isn't that right, Brady?" As I've mentioned in the section about introducing a kitten to a cat, you can also refer to the newcomer as, for example, Brady's cat.

INTRODUCING A THIRD CAT OR KITTEN

A third party can sometimes cause the triangle syndrome in which two cats treat the third as the scape-cat. If you have two cats and one cat is your shadow or prefers to be a Greta Garbo "I-want-to-be-alone" type and you think the other cat needs a playmate, a spunky kitten or young adolescent might be the answer. But try to adopt one that appears to be cat oriented, so it will befriend your cats before it reaches out to people. Choose a male if you have two females, and a female if you have two males. You can choose either sex if you already have one of each.

You might want to choose a cat or kitten who has similar coloring to the cat that you feel needs a companion. Your cat will recognize the color by scent, and the familiarity will be a plus to the relationship. If either of your cats has had a problem with a particular color or breed of cat, it's best to avoid such a cat.

Use my method of how to introduce a kitten to a cat for the best results (see pages 111–115). If it turns out that the newcomer is not the right answer for your two guys, find the newcomer a new home where he will blossom. You can consider you did a good deed and acted as a halfway house for this particular cat or kitten.

A PUPPY OR DOG FOR YOUR CAT

It's been just you and your three-year-old female cat, but now you think you'd like to adopt a dog or maybe even a puppy. Your cat seems bored and perhaps even frustrated. You work long hours, and she doesn't have much company. You think a dog might be the answer to her loneliness. You know of a reliable dog walker and some weekends you travel to the country, where the three of you could have a very pleasant time. A co-worker also has a dog trainer. But you can't decide if you should adopt a puppy or a dog and you don't know which sex would be preferable.

If your cat is playful and adventurous, you might opt for a male or female puppy of at least three months. But a cat-oriented dog—one that's lived happily with cats—would probably be a good match and would not involve the expense of a puppy. Furthermore, an older dog would be housebroken and much easier to discipline and manage. Be sure to adopt a dog that's neutered or spayed and has a clean bill of health. Finally a dog of similar coloring to your cat would seem familiar because your cat can determine color by scent.

Match Your Cat's Catsonality

Here are some general guidelines to help you select the appropriate dog or puppy for your cat.

- If your female cat is over four years old and not dog oriented, choose a dog of about three to six years old with a mellow and gentle dogsonality. You don't want her to be intimidated by a dynamo dog.

- If you have an extroverted cat that's dog friendly, a young puppy would suit.

- A sedate male cat over four years old should be coupled with a gentle female dog.

- A timid, young cat should do well with a calm dog or puppy of either sex.

- If your cat is acquainted with dogs, try to select the type of dog with whom she's had good experiences—not the type that agitated her.

- If either cat or dog is sexually mature and needs to be neutered or spayed, arrange the introduction for at least two weeks after the surgery. (See Matching Catsonality Types, pages 109–110, for additional tips.)

Match Your Kitten's Catsonality

Your kitten should be at least three months old before you adopt a dog or puppy to avoid any accidental injuries.

- If your kitten is shy and dogs are an unknown commodity, select a calm and relaxed puppy or dog.

- If your kitten is dog or puppy shy because of a traumatic episode, don't plunge into the adoption of either. After the dust really settles, invite a friend over with her dog or puppy on a leash to see what your cat's reaction is. Don't invite a dog or puppy that is similar in color or disposition to the one that traumatized your kitten.

- You might prefer to adopt a puppy, so he can grow up with your kitten. But if your kitten keeps you hopping, a dog might be easier to tolerate.

- A type-A catsonality would probably do well with a playful but generous dog or puppy.

Preliminaries for the Dog's or Puppy's Arrival

1. Familiarize your cat or kitten with the newcomer with tapes of a dog barking. Start off with short sequences so it won't be a total shock. Let him become slowly accustomed to the new sound. Don't turn the volume up too loud because a feline is noise sensitive. As the tape plays, stroke your cat or engage him in play so he forms a secure and happy association with the sound. To prevent fear or apprehension, tell him what a great cat or kitten he is.

2. Trim your cat or kitten's claws so he won't scratch your new animal.

3. Select a high feeding place for your cat or kitten so the newcomer can't devour his food. Create a situation that prevents a territorial tug-of-war.

4. Provide your kitten with a high, comfy perch so he can retreat from the newcomer at will.

5. The litter box should be placed where the newcomer can't gain access. A covered box would work if it's acceptable to your cat or kitten.

6. Dog-proof your cat's toys by placing them in a basket on his high perch. He can choose to play with them whenever he likes. Now and again the newcomer may score, but you'll prevent total destruction with this precaution. Hopefully, the newcomer will prefer his own toys and/or obedience training will curb this temptation.

Introduction Day (or Look, Don't Touch)

1. Don't act as the newcomer's escort. You don't want your cat or kitten to feel betrayed. Choose an escort that hasn't befriended him.

2. When the escort enters, you and your cat or kitten should be sequestered in another room.

3. If you're getting a puppy, the escort can introduce him in a crate or kennel and leave it in a corner of the room. You might do the same if you bring home a small dog.

4. If you're getting a dog or large puppy, if possible, he should be kept in a separate room with his creature comforts. (If not, keep him on a leash so your cat or kitten isn't threatened. You don't want to cultivate fear.) Use a gate or screen that the newcomer can't jump over to divide the room. They'll be able to view each other without physical contact.

5. After the escort has positioned the newcomer, you and your cat or kitten can enter.

6. *Don't* force or entice him to encounter the newcomer. Allow it to be your cat's choice.

7. You and the escort can settle down to a chatty visit. Try to talk about other subjects. Remember a cat likes to feel he's in charge and not dictated to or influenced by your actions.

8. If you're not too nervous, arrange to go out for a few hours. But be sure to have the newcomer safely and securely positioned in a separate room, or at least a crate, so your cat is not at risk of an incident or accident.

9. Arrange for someone to walk the newcomer for the first few days if he's old enough to go outdoors. Your cat or kitten will accept the newcomer more quickly if you have little contact with the newcomer.

10. Refrain from exciting the newcomer so your cat or kitten isn't overwhelmed by his high energy.

11. If you're able to separate them, switch territories every few days. This will reduce territorial spats because it will allow each to get a good whiff of the other.

Avoid Transitional Stress

Whenever you must interact with the newcomer say comforting things, such as, "I'm going to feed your dog" or "I'll walk your puppy so you don't have to do it." This technique will prevent your cat or kitten's feeling jealous. Think of these announcements as a bridge to happy interactions.

The Merry Encounter

The day of your cat's first encounter with the dog should be one where you're relaxed and light spirited. At this point your animals should have exhibited signs of general acceptance and toleration. If there's still a lot of tension, wait until they're more at ease with each other and curious in a friendly manner. The following guidelines will simplify the encounter:

- Remove the gate or screen so they can roam at will and confront each other.

- Keep your interference to a minimum so they can proceed at their own speed.

- Distract them with a few words of enthusiasm or a spritz of water from the plant mister if they become too excited.

- Return them to their respective territories to avoid any possible accidents whenever you leave home. Continue this precaution until you're confident of their interactions.

- Remember, the more relaxed you are, the more quickly they will accept each other.

- Have visitors provide the newcomer with attention so your contact is limited and your cat or kitten feels less threatened. This will hasten their bond.

Sundry Tips

- The introduction of a dog or puppy to a kitten, rather than a cat, may involve less repetition of strategy because a kitten is usually more flexible than a cat.

- Sometimes it is best to use sedation for the dog and/ or cat if the anxiety level is high.

- Remember, your cat or kitten should be doted on to prevent any insecurity—even if you have to ardently pursue him!

- An outdoor cat may accept the newcomer more quickly because of his independence and extended territory.

- Quite frequently a cat will accept a dog with less hesitation than he would another cat, because his own species can be more of a threat.

Happy Ending

Don't be surprised if your cat or kitten works out an approved living arrangement with the newcomer within the next few weeks—or even sooner. Genuine camaraderie is the goal, but tolerance may be their choice. An outdoor cat may choose to accompany the newcomer on his walks. Finally, don't be surprised if the newcomer decides to groom your cat's head and face.

Upsets are to be expected. They go with the territory. But the love and companionship of the newcomer will outweigh the upsets.

A CAT OR KITTEN FOR YOUR DOG OR PUPPY

You've always been a dog person, but you realize that your dog could use some companionship. A second dog would probably be best for him, but you don't want another dog and he already has dog friends he plays with when you take him to the park. Your neighbor has a cat and dog. They have a terrific relationship, and you've become quite fond of this cat. Perhaps a cat or kitten would be the best companion for your dog.

Match Your Dog's or Puppy's Dogsonality

- A kitten should be at least three months old to prevent its being accidentally injured by the puppy or dog.

- Choose a large, energetic kitten if your dog or puppy is large.

- A mellow cat or kitten would suit a timid or reclusive dog or puppy. An older dog might also do best with such a newcomer.

- A high-energy dog or puppy should have a newcomer that won't be overwhelmed by his exuberance.

- If either party is sexually mature, arrange to have him or her neutered or spayed at least two weeks before introduction.

- Avoid a type of cat or kitten with which your dog or puppy has experienced unfriendly interactions. Comply with his gender preference.

- A dog- or puppy-oriented cat or kitten would be a plus.

Introducing a Cat or Kitten to Your Dog

BEFORE THE INTRODUCTION DAY

1. Both animals should have a clean bill of health.

2. If the newcomer is unaccustomed to dogs, whenever possible acquaint him with a dog's bark by use of an audio- or videotape. Talk and stroke the newcomer while you listen to the tape to form a friendly association.

3. Present your dog or puppy with one of the newcomer's objects (for example, a favorite toy) so the newcomer's scent will be familiar.

4. Arrange to feed the newcomer on a high perch that the dog or puppy can't reach.

5. Purchase a scratching post for the newcomer. A covered litter box is advisable if the box is accessible to your dog or puppy.

6. The newcomer's claws should be trimmed.

INTRODUCTION DAY

You can assume the role of escort to the newcomer because a dog usually responds well to authority and command. Your dog or puppy will be influenced by your acceptance of the newcomer. But don't try to manipulate or force the two together. The following steps will ease the process:

1. The newcomer should be presented in a see-through carrier. Place it in a spot where they can observe each other at a healthy distance.

2. Present the newcomer with an object that has your puppy or dog's scent.

3. After they've become aware of each other, move the newcomer's carrier to a room where you have set up the litter box. Close the door so the newcomer has privacy.

4. Use a gate or screen to separate the two, but the newcomer's comforts should be within his area.

5. Switch their territories every few days for short intervals so they'll become acquainted with each other's scent.

6. Leave it up to the newcomer to decide when to join his new companion.

7. You can have contact with the newcomer even before the two bond. But don't ignore your dog or puppy! He was your first companion. Indulge him so he doesn't become resentful of the newcomer. Mention his name whenever you interact with the newcomer so he feels included and in control.

THE ENCOUNTER

If the two haven't already connected, select a day when you are feeling cheery and relaxed.

1. Remove the gate or screen so there's easy access.

2. Don't interfere! It's their relationship. But if their actions make you nervous, use a plant mister or your voice to separate them. Try to stay calm and collected so they don't sense your angst.

3. Separate them when you leave home. You should do this by replacing the screen or gate. Repeat this until you are very sure of their behavior.

4. Use sedation if either animal appears overstressed.

5. You can interact with the newcomer, but dote on your dog or puppy so he doesn't feel left out.

GRAND OUTCOME

Within a few weeks the two should have bonded in a loving or at least tolerant manner. Don't be surprised if the newcomer becomes top banana!

OTHER ANIMALS AND YOUR CAT

Guinea Pigs or Hamsters

A rodent may entertain your cat, but you must take the utmost caution to protect such an animal. Your cat may think it is his next meal or new play toy, and there could be a catastrophe. To prevent this, the rodent should be housed in a cat-proof environment. If your cat becomes too excited or anxious with the newcomer, you may have to rethink your plan. You don't want your cat to become frustrated because he can't devour the new addition. But if your cat is fascinated and intrigued, the presence of the new animal may be all right.

Tropical Fish

Some cats are soothed by the presence of an inhabited aquarium or fish bowl. Your cat may be pleased by such company. But make certain the habitat is cat proof.

Birds

Hang the cage from a high, secure place that your cat can't possibly reach. Whenever you have to care for the bird or decide to allow it to have an outing, your cat should be securely ensconced in another room. Don't risk any foul play. It may be that your cat will befriend the bird, but don't make assumptions.

If the newcomer is a sturdy, cat-wise parrot, your cat may not even consider such a bird as potential game. He may even show it respect.

Rabbits or Ferrets

Provide a cat-proof abode for the rabbit or ferret so your cat can observe it without physical contact. You should sequester your cat when you let the newcomer out of his cage until you're confident that your cat is rabbit or ferret friendly. Until that time you might want to set up a screen door or full-length gate so the two can view each other but not interact. When your cat becomes buddies with the newcomer, don't be surprised if they share the same litter box. But even so, two litter boxes make it even steven.

Your Cat and His New Housemate

Because a kitten is usually more flexible than a cat, a kitten will probably accept a newcomer more rapidly than a cat will. But whether you have a kitten or cat, it's important that you verbally include them in your interactions with the newcomer. Let them know your intentions before your interaction with the newcomer. "I'm going to feed the newcomer so he doesn't eat your food or so you don't have to do it" is an example. Your cat or kitten will get the feeling of camaraderie and control by your tone of voice and your body posture. Because he's included, he'll feel less threatened. When you speak to the newcomer, mention your cat or kitten's name, saying, for example, "Isn't that right, Kitten?" However, because the newcomer is a different species, the element of competition is usually less than when two cats live in the same household.

There are sure to be some tense or upset moments, but very soon your cat or kitten will have his own chum and you'll enjoy the love and companionship you receive from both.

Aggression, Feuding, Timidity, and Overgrooming

ANXIETY AND YOUR CAT

You can't imagine why your cat's behavior is suddenly out of line. He's always been quirky, but now his behavior is more than odd—it's annoying, frustrating, and sometimes abusive. It used to be periodic, but now it seems to be his signature. What's wrong with him? Is he neurotic? What causes this deviant behavior and will there ever be an end to it?

A cat's behavior may become deviant or uncatlike when he feels threatened or frustrated. This feeling can be manifested in anxious and neurotic behavior. If the feeling lingers, such behavior will continue or reoccur. But if the problem can be isolated and defined at the onset, therapeutic measures can release the anxiety within a short time.

A Cry for Help

A cat can have an uncomfortable reaction to separation from his people or companions or anxiety about a new companion or person in his home, a change in residence, the onset of sexual maturity, the single cat syndrome, or other situations that trouble or threaten him.

The anxiety from these stress-activated feelings is communicated to you by his deviant or abnormal behavior as a cry for help.

Unfamiliarity

It's because a cat becomes so used to his routine and that which is familiar (unless he decides to change his script) that when the pattern changes, his behavior deviates from the norm. His reaction can trigger acute and long-term problems, especially if he lacks self-esteem.

Self-esteem

Self-esteem is one of the most important elements in a catsonality. It begins the moment the mother cat conceives. Healthy, socialized parents kick off a well-integrated kitten. The development continues during kittenhood and is reinforced later in every phase of a cat's life. A healthy relationship with the mother cat, positive interactions with littermates, and stable, loving relationships with humans are the ingredients that affect a cat's good feeling about himself. They provide a sense of security. If any of these early relationships is dysfunctional, a cat becomes a vulnerable target for ongoing anxiety or stress. It's the cat's ability to cope with this stress that affects his catsonality and changes his behavior.

Low Self-esteem Can Trigger a Low Stress Tolerance

Low self-esteem may cause a cat to become an emotional sponge. You could refer to him as a thin-skinned or emotionally fragile cat. His tolerance for stress will be lower, so he will probably have a stronger reaction when he feels frustrated or anxious. A thicker-skinned cat usually has a higher tolerance of stress (see also Chapter 5). That's why one cat can withstand a multitude of stressful events and another can become totally undone.

An emotionally thin-skinned cat reacts strongly to changes in his environment and often mirrors his person's behavior. Sometimes the reaction is immediate, and other times it is delayed.

Delayed Reaction

When the reaction to previous stress is delayed and apparently out of context to the present situation, your cat's unacceptable behavior totally baffles you. You wonder why he is suddenly out of line when everything has been so calm for days—until you remember the turmoil you were in three weeks before. Unacceptable behavior is easier to understand when there's direct cause and effect.

Unresolved Insecurity

A severe reaction to stress can sometimes trigger acute and long-term problems, especially when a catsonality is extremely fragile. The pervasive, unresolved insecurity deep inside the cat can surface and linger when he is threatened. When this occurs, it may be necessary to integrate new coping mechanisms so that he will be a happier and healthier cat (see Chapter 5). Otherwise, the so-called blocks will continue to perpetuate neurotic behavior. The sooner the problem is isolated, the sooner therapeutic measures can be used to release the anxiety and sustain the cat's ability to cope in a comfortable way.

AGGRESSION IN RESPONSE TO ANXIETY

You have one cat, a neutered, ten-month-old male, and you wonder why he has become physically abusive to you. He's always been saucy and his love nips are his trademark, but now he's become totally aggressive. His neurotic behavior is downright abusive. He ambushes you out of nowhere. Yesterday he even nipped your cheek when you were stretched out on the sofa. He seems to think you're another cat.

Single-cat Syndrome

He interacts with you as he would another cat because he's frustrated. Another cat might very well be your solution to his neurotic behavior. Nip it in the bud! Don't let him continue to be a victim of the single-cat syndrome. But if a second cat is out of the question, you might want to consider getting another animal of a different species to keep him company. Chapter 8 discusses how to introduce other animals to your cat.

The objective is to assist your cat with his need for attention and exercise. You don't want his neurotic or deviant behavior to become a habit.

If you can't accommodate him with an animal companion, try one of the following solutions:

- Give him longer play periods but make sure you don't stop them while he's going strong. Wind down slowly so he shifts into low gear. You don't want to increase his frustration. To prevent anxiety from building up, let him know when you're moving on to a new activity. Otherwise the angst builds, and you have the ripple effect, especially with a cat that already exhibits anxious behavior.

- Arrange for a neighbor to visit your cat. A young, responsible child who's a cat lover might provide the ideal playmate for your frustrated cat. A child usually has enough passion and creativity to challenge and amuse a cat.

- Hire a professional cat sitter to add variety to your cat's agenda and amuse him at times when you are at work or otherwise unavailable.

- Arrange play dates with a neighbor's cat if both cats are receptive.

- Borrow a cat-friendly dog.

When the inner stress or anxiety is quickly discharged and/or satisfied, your cat's discomfort will disappear. But prolonged anxiety can turn into constant fear or timidity, threatening a cat's peace of mind and physical well-being. The fear and timidity exacerbated by low self-esteem can trigger acute and long-term disorders. If your cat is exhibiting unusually aggressive behavior, don't ignore it in the hope that it will go away!

Long-term Aggression and Cat Feuds

When a cat is threatened and his fear escalates, he resorts to fight or flight. Flight is usually less offensive to humans, but fight can be harmful to both the cat and his source of anxiety. The source can be a companion animal or person.

DISPLACED OR REDIRECTED AGGRESSION

Sometimes an anxious cat who has become aggressive will attack a neutral person or cat companion in reaction to a particular trauma. This trauma could be the result of an alien cat or interloper, a loud noise, or anxiety or hysteria of a companion cat.

POSSIBLE SCENARIO

One day your younger cat's head became caught in the handles of a shopping bag. He tore around the room, entangled in the bag, before you could rescue him. As you reassured him, your other cat came over and started to growl. You quickly distracted them. Yet you worry that it will be months before your cats bury the hatchet. What do you do?

Distraction is the answer when the cats will obey you. But if not, separation should provide the needed time to recover from the anxiety. If after a few hours of separation there is still tension, once again separate the cats. Don't forget to include creature comforts and try to be as relaxed as possible so your tension doesn't add to the mix.

YO-YO SYNDROME

You thought the storm had passed because, despite a few minor blowups, your guys were seemingly their old selves. But three weeks later, the fur began to fly. Once again, you separated them, but unlike before they showed no signs of purr and make up. You felt you couldn't separate them forever, so what are you to do? No matter what set them off, you knew deep down that somehow they had to become stronger so they wouldn't be vulnerable to other loaded situations.

As you might guess, whatever set them off again is almost immaterial. What's urgent is that you provide the environment where they can regroup and cope so they won't be the target of each other's tension. The following tips will help to defuse the tension and start them on the way to regaining their old relationship:

1. Rule out a medical problem. Take both cats in for a physical exam to make sure no malady instigated or contributed to the angst.

2. It's important that both cats see each other without physical contact. To establish this, separate them with a screen or Plexiglas door. You can also use sliding window screens in a doorway. Measure the height and width of the door frame to determine how many screens you will need. The screens can be fastened to the door frame with adhesive Velcro. When you need to gain entrance, you can temporarily remove the bottom screen.

3. A few days after you have arranged this setup, move each cat's food and water dishes a short distance from the barrier so they can confront each other without physical contact.

4. Each cat should have his particular creature comforts.

5. If your cats generally sleep with you, perhaps you can accommodate each on alternate nights.

6. Remove a catalyst. Sometimes a neutral feline or other companion can be the catalyst for the hostility. However, the catalyst doesn't always have to be the target of their aggression.

7. Whenever you interact with one cat, even if the other cat is out of sight, mention the latter's name so he'll feel included. You want to be a unit moving along in tandem in order to prevent jealousy on either cat's part.

8. To avoid transitional angst, which can lead to more tension, verbalize any sudden change of motion.

Your cats may not understand you, but this will help to keep your cats in sync with your change of actions and reduce the startle effect. An example is: "I'm answering the phone, going into the bedroom now, opening the closet."

9. Arrange to spend some quiet time near the barrier. This might involve reading a book or letter, or interacting with any object that makes you feel good. Your cats will be soothed by your low-key energy. The more relaxed they are, the less tense they will be.

PLAY TIME

When you feel that they are tolerant enough of each other, you can try to engage them in play. Open the barrier a crack and dangle a toy (their favorite) or string to each of them. If this is successful, repeat this for a few days. Next, try dangling the same object from one to the other. If this is a source of anxiety, return to using the two objects. Use your judgment as to when to alternate one object between them. This technique helps to build their tolerance of each other.

Initial Encounter

Once you have established that they can peacefully cope with each other in this limited capacity, you can open the barrier a crack so they can gain entry to the other's space. But don't push them. Sit back on a comfy sofa or rug and occupy yourself with something that relaxes and/ or amuses you. Turn on some soft music. The cats may choose to stay put and possibly sniff each other. A few hisses are fine, but if there's too much tension, close the barrier. If they decide to interact in the same territory, don't extend their interaction for more than twenty minutes. But if there's a dispute, distract and return them to their respective territories. Don't try to get in the middle if there's a feud, and spray them with water from a plant mister to cool them off. Lure them back with a favorite toy or small treat. Be sure to secure the barrier.

SUBSEQUENT ENCOUNTERS

When there have been a series of harmonious twenty-minute sessions, extend the time to an hour. After they've adjusted to this, you might even leave for half an hour. If this period alone together was peaceful, repeat and slowly extend your time away from home. You can tell whether they've been happy together by their reactions when you return home. Don't be in a hurry or you'll make it hard for them to build increased tolerance of each other.

SETBACK

If there's a feud, don't give up! They're stronger now and will recover quickly. Don't let them meet for the next few days. This will allow them time to regroup. Their next encounter should be a good one. But if there's an incident, it means they need more time. Remember, it's important that you stay relaxed so you can give them the confidence they need. Perhaps a cat-friendly neighbor can help by interacting with one while you concentrate on the other.

TIME FRAME FOR RECOVERY

The mending process may take about three months or longer. Each cat progresses at his own speed. You can only provide the "right" environment to assist their recovery. Try very hard to see light at the end of the tunnel so your confidence is contagious.

AUXILIARY AID

It's frequently necessary to provide auxiliary support so your cats' recovery is shorter and more comfortable. The veterinarian may want to prescribe a psychotropic drug, such as Valium, Prozac, BuSpar or Elavil. In my experience I have had the most success with Valium, and it has been used longer on cats than the other drugs listed. But that does not totally rule out the others' reliability. One cat's tonic can be another's toxin. Hormonal therapy is also sometimes effective, but its long-term use can often trigger medical complications. Drug therapy should not be forever, but should be used carefully, slowly decreased, and finally stopped. Sometimes it may be necessary to give a cat medication again when potentially stressful situations are anticipated. But this usually involves short-term use. It's usually best to medicate both cats, or the victim's angst will continue to trigger the offender's aggression.

Homeopathic remedies are another source of auxiliary and alternate relief. There are homeopathic veterinarians and also homeopaths who treat people but who can also offer expert advice on how to treat a cat. Homeopathic remedies are generally not as powerful as synthetic drugs and take longer to kick in but are said to be less toxic and with side effects that are relatively minimal.

Music therapy is another easy way to diminish stress and tension. Soft radio music or a tape or CD of your favorite selections should soothe all of you. If your cats are responsive to touch, massage therapy will help to release the tension. As the body relaxes, the mind will follow (see Chapter 10).

General Misconceptions About Your Anxious or Aggressive Cat

Fiction: A cat who's started on drug therapy for misbehavior will become addicted.

Fact: If the particular drug is properly prescribed and used in conjunction with a behavioral therapy program to integrate new coping mechanisms to relieve anxiety, the drug can be slowly discontinued. However, such a drug used with no therapy for major emotional and behavioral problems will generally lose its potency while the problems will continue.

Fiction: Once a cat has a serious feud with a companion, there's no hope of a truce.

Fact: Time, patience, and proper behavioral modification can mend the relationship. There is every reason to hope for a truce, although the cats may not return to their past level of devotion. On the other hand, sometimes the relationship becomes even tighter after the kinks are worked out.

Fiction: Two cats that have lived together and bonded should never be split up, even if they are now bitter enemies. You love them too much to make such a decision.

Fact: If reconciliation appears out of the question, you must do what's best for the welfare of the cats. With a careful search, a loving person can be located to adopt whichever cat seems most likely to blossom in a new living situation. Console yourself with the prospect that you can visit your former cat in a happy environment. Perhaps you can later couple the cat that remains in your life with a new companion. You can address such an issue down the road.

Fiction: You don't know what the catalyst was that wreaked havoc with your cats, so it will be impossible to solve the problem.

Fact: Even if you can't identify the source of discontent, you can still provide treatment to clear the air. The reconstructive techniques that I've described will offer them the support they need to increase their tolerance of potentially stressful situations. The source that ignited their rift might even surface during their recovery.

Remember: It's important not to treat only symptoms, and reconstructive therapy is the essential ingredient for diminishing the fear and sustaining the security and confidence needed to cope comfortably day to day.

When Your Cat Attacks People

Now and again your cat has taken a nip or two out of various visitors, and he's not always careful with his claws. But the assaults have never been enough to worry you. You've always enjoyed his spirit. His victims toed the line if they made a return visit or you gave him his own room if they were skeptical. He's always been great with your other cat who idolizes him. But last week he drew blood from your neighbor, and it was hours before you could approach him. You might have been his next victim if you didn't keep your distance. Even now you're wary about his behavior. What can you do to relieve him of this angst and stop his behavior that once was acceptable but now is dangerous?

PEOPLE AS VICTIMS

People have become your cat's tension targets. What gets you is that this attack-cat behavior is totally unpredictable. That is, sometimes you can figure it out but at other times it seems totally out of nowhere. Your cat is emotionally unstable, and a particular event or person reawakens a residual feeling of angst. He attacks, trying to get the enemy before the enemy gets him. His behavior may appear a bit psychotic, but his behavior is a direct reaction to his reality. Unless his fear eventually abates, he will continue the attack-cat mode when he feels out of control. As I've explained earlier in this chapter, if a cat's early kittenhood has been a traumatic one, unresolved angst or fear may surface when he feels threatened, and his behavior will reflect his fear. The following program will help to abate this residual angst so you and your cat can live a healthier and happier life.

REHAB PROGRAM FOR ATTACK CATS

- Take him to the vet for a physical exam to rule out any medical problems. If your cat is wary of veterinary hospitals, you might want to arrange a house call. However, schedule this visit after he has recovered from his anxiety attack. A medical problem may have contributed to his aggressive outburst or could be a result of his deviant behavior.

- After your cat has had an attack-cat episode, it is usually best to keep him quiet so he doesn't become overstimulated. You don't want to provoke another attack. Even if he appears calm, internally he may still be rattled. You might want to fix up a basket or out-of-the-way sunny spot for him to hang out in. Sometimes a cat carrier can provide such a retreat. But you should fill it with tissue paper or something that he prefers to nestle in.

- If your cat has a companion, you might want to separate them temporarily—unless your anxious cat craves his companion's company.

- Try not to have visitors for the next two weeks. If this isn't possible, sequester your cat with his creature comforts when visitors drop by. Escort him to his retreat in a protective manner so he doesn't feel punished.

- It's not unusual for an anxious cat to be noise sensitive. You can modify this if you lower the volume of your telephone's ring, doorbell, and television. You might also want to purchase an environmental muffler, such as a white-noise machine. Soft music or an audiotape of ocean, rain, and other soothing sounds will add to this tranquility.

- Try to arrange two or three daily periods of ten minutes of quiet time with your cat. This will help to increase his relaxation.

- As he becomes calmer, you can allow him short play periods. Stop if he becomes too excited. Remember to slow down your body language as you wind down his play. He is very affected by your actions.

- As his tolerance increases, you can give him a pinch of catnip to work out his pent-up energy. It usually produces a mellow response. Your cat will probably become very energetic, and the release of energy will help to relax him. I like to think of it as a jog through the park, punctuated with a few healthy stretches and a contented feeling.

- If a particular person is your cat's tension target, wait until your cat appears to be on the emotional rebound before the two have an encounter. Be sure to mention your cat's name as you converse with the person. But this encounter shouldn't occur until the person also feels secure. You might want to hold your cat on your lap for the first meeting, and make sure it is a brief one.

- If your cat is especially anxious, it may be necessary to sequester him. If space is at a premium, a large dog carrier or crate with his creature comforts is an option.

- He can have supervised forays in the rest of your house when you feel he can cope with the added space. *Remember:* When a cat is frightened or insecure, he usually seeks shelter in a secluded nook. It's important to realize that your cat is frightened inside, and his aggressive behavior has been a symptom of this feeling. You must make the decision to give him the solace he needs to overcome this inner fear. Once your cat realizes that he is safe in his designated space, it will become a source of comfort and security to him. Don't fret if he's reluctant and agitated at the start.

- Your cat is affected by his diet, so make certain it is not a source of agitation. Certain foods can increase or decrease his emotional/physical comfort. Discuss your cat's nutrition with your vet.

- If a drug is used as auxiliary therapy, the behavioral program should be continued and modified slowly even after the drug has been stopped.

- Do things to nurture yourself. Any exercise or activity that you can do at home that tickles your fancy will usually please your cat.

- If your cat has a setback, don't despair! He's a lot stronger than he was before and he will quickly recover from this incident.

The more confident you can be about his recovery, the easier it will be for him to take the leap. Otherwise your insecurity will influence his response. You don't want your cat to mirror your lack of belief. Tell him he's getting better. Because with your help, he is!

TIMIDITY

A timid cat is often one who was neglected as a kitten by his mother cat. This can make him very fearful of new situations. If he becomes very traumatized, his health and spirit may be compromised. Generally, it's easier to live with a cat who flees when he feels threatened rather than with a cat who charges to meet the enemy. But if such a cat has too many fearful episodes, his behavior could become a major problem. Usually such a cat seeks the protection of a companion cat whom he adores. But even with such an anchor, a traumatic incident can sometimes wreak havoc with this fragile cat. The more you can do to increase his tolerance of everyday life, the healthier he will be (see Chapter 14).

NOCTURNAL ANGST AND SLEEPLESS NIGHTS

You never thought of yourself as a fidgety sleeper. In fact you can usually catch a few winks wherever you are whenever you feel the need. But your cat has put an end to your great adaptability. He ran over your body and poked at your face with his paw. Perhaps it was a houseguest who annoyed him, and his behavior was a delayed reaction to the irritation. Or it could be that he misses your former beau, or that you've been out too much. It may even be that his behavior is a reaction to your inner turmoil about your present work situation. Whatever it is that has him unhinged, it has to be squared away. You need your sleep!

How to curb your cat's antisleep campaign:
- Take him to the vet for a medical exam. You want to make sure there's no physical reason for his antics. A cardiac or thyroid disorder can cause a cat to be-

come agitated and meow or howl because he feels uncomfortable and disoriented. You should also consult his veterinarian about nutrition to be certain a vitamin deficiency isn't the cause of his wild performance.

• Tire him out with an evening game of chase if he's been a couch potato all day. You want him to release that energy while you're up and about—not when you're trying to sleep.

• Give him catnip. It may help to work out his bottled-up energy. Once the catnip relaxes him, a few hugs should channel any stored-up tension.

• A bedtime snack will warm his tummy and soothe his spirit. But if your cat's a pudgette, trim his dinner a smidgen so the snack doesn't break the scale.

Wee Hours Vigil

Some nights he's an angel, and it's not until the wee hours that his vigilante vigil begins. Food can remedy his wakefulness, but at this rate breakfast could get earlier and earlier. Other times there is little you can do to protect your sleep. He kneads on your chest, licks your face, plays hockey with your hair, rustles the blinds, or does a little of each. It all adds up to sleep deprivation, and you don't want to lose any more winks. Why doesn't he get the hint?

Ways to combat your cat's nightly vigil:

• Try a sharp "no" to stop his noise-making. Remember to say, "Good!" when he stops. A spritz of water from the plant mister might also cool him off.

• As he rubs against you, grab him and hold him next to you. Breathe freely. Relax your body and stroke him so he will forget his hunger pangs or whatever else is bothering him.

- Entice him to hang out under the covers. This hide-away may provide the distraction he needs to calm down.

- If he is misbehaving because he is hungry, and his wake-up time is before yours, prepare his breakfast at bedtime so it's ready for him in the morning. But after you prepare it and tuck it away, give him a snack so he's not confused and frustrated.

The Final Showdown

You've tried many of the aforementioned suggestions. But suppose they don't work? Why hasn't this commotion ended, and what can you now do to stop it?

It may be that your cat has some deep-down angst that he must express when you're least able to cope with it. It could be that your biological rhythm during the night, and especially near waking time, excites him. Even small changes, such as a few tosses and turns, may affect his sleep. This could cause him to appear at the door with several meows and scoot across your body. If he's bedded down with you, he may act in a way that ends your slumber. The following steps should calm him and help to restore your sleep:

- Mix ¼ teaspoon of chamomile tea leaves in a small ball of tasty food or vitamin gel. This tea is known to soothe and relax. It can be his evening or bedtime snack.

- When bedtime arrives, take him to a room with his creature comforts. Do this in a gentle manner so he doesn't feel that he is being punished. Soft radio music or an audiotape will keep him company. (See

Chapter 10. As you leave the room, breathe freely, smile, and tell him you'll see him later. If he has a companion, it's best to sequester the two of them. This space will provide the play area he needs and won't interfere with your nocturnal plans. The first few nights he may meow a bit or knock a few things about, so you may want to cat-proof the space. But as each night passes, he'll accept this as his bedtime sanctuary. Don't feel guilty about this arrangement. Remind yourself that his previous bedtime agenda bred mutual frustration and resentment. This new plan will help mend your relationship.

- Your cat may need an anti-anxiety drug to ease his angst. For a while, you may have to give it to him daily and in conjunction with the steps I've mentioned to increase his capacity to tolerate uncomfortable situations. You will need a prescription unless you decide to use an over-the-counter medication such as valerian root, which you can purchase from a health food store.

- You could try homeopathic remedies, which are composed of minute doses of substances that in a large dose would create the symptoms of the disease that's to be cured. The Bach flower remedies are made from ingredients of flowering plants, trees, and specially treated waters.

- Acupuncture, acupressure, the T-touch, massage, and Chinese herbs can also be used to relieve your cat's angst. Linda Tellington Jones, an animal trainer, created a "touch therapy" that uses her fingers or a Heat and Sound Soother in a circular motion to relax animals. But whichever remedy you decide to use for your cat, consult an expert for the best results.

- If you tend to be an insomniac, a musical relaxation tape or a sleep-sound appliance that creates sounds, such as waterfalls, ocean waves, and birds, should lull both of you to sleep.

INDISCRIMINATE EATING AND GROOMING OR OBSESSIVE-COMPULSIVE SYNDROME

You have two cats that are absolutely the light of your life. But there's a big wrinkle that you'd give anything to see ironed out. Your two cats have a terrific relationship, but every now and again they become jealous of each other. This is often when the trouble begins. One cat overgrooms himself until he has bald spots—usually on his tummy. His target used to be his tail, which he mutilated so badly that the tip had to be amputated. Your other cat has eaten parts of woolen socks, sweaters, panty hose, string, and even paper. A plastic toothpick even became lodged in his intestines so that he had to have emergency surgery. This is no way to live. How can you curb your cats' inappropriate grooming and eating?

These types of deviant behavior are often symptoms of low self-esteem and fear, such as the other behavior discussed in this chapter. But unlike the previous misbehavior, which was sadistic, this is masochistic. When a cat feels threatened and he doesn't release his anxiety quickly, he may begin to behave in a self-destructive way. Such obsessive-compulsive behavior becomes the outlet for the cat's discomfort. Both grooming and eating are healthy, catlike behaviors until they become habits or rituals.

A cat will occasionally ingest a particular object he shouldn't, and this isn't always dangerous. It's also easy to keep such objects out of sight (see Chapter 2). Also, a cat can become overzealous about his grooming. But he can be easily distracted when this occurs. However, when these habits persist, a cat's health is endangered. The sooner protective and preventive steps are taken, the shorter his recovery period will be.

The following section will deal with more severe manifestations of your cats' anxiety caused by fear, low self-esteem, and other catalysts.

Pica

If your cat has an appetite for eating nonedible things (referred to as *pica*), it's usually a combination of anxiety and his enjoyment of texture and/or taste of particular chemicals that creates this addiction. You can help your cat kick this bugaboo by taking away objects he favors. Otherwise he's constantly tempted. Once he gets a taste of the particular object he likes, his mouth is off and running. When he becomes overstimulated (happy, sad), he becomes more vulnerable and, thus, more apt to indulge his addiction. You might compare your cat's habit to a person's excessive need for alcohol, sweets, or cigarettes.

If your cat is attracted to large objects, such as your sofa or chairs, it's easier to remove your cat than to remove these objects. Therefore, if you suspect your cat will panic when you are out of the home, sequester your cat with his creature comforts in an area that does not have these objects. Follow the same procedure if your cat becomes panicked when you're home.

Alopecia Nervosa

Incessant grooming or biting to the extent of baldness or mutilation is referred to as *alopecia nervosa*. Grooming is a feline ritual. A cat often grooms when he is doubtful or agitated because it produces a feeling of comfort and reminds him of his mother cat. When he becomes anxious or excited, he may fixate on a certain spot to wash. Because it's been sensitized, this area may then begin to itch or tingle. Your cat licks the spot again, trying to remove or reduce the discomfort. His behavior becomes compulsive.

Soon, there's a self-perpetuating physical problem that may require minor surgery. Generally, the proper medication (an oral or injectable type of cortisone) can reduce the inflammation and discomfort—especially if given at the onset of an attack. An Elizabethan collar is commonly used to prevent contact with your cat's irritated area.

Steps to Recovery

MEDICAL EXAM

It's vital to rule out any physiological problem with a thorough medical exam. Your cat could be allergic to something in his diet, and that could cause him to overgroom and/or to indiscriminately ingest. Another cause could be a neurological disorder that sometimes results in seizures. Excessive washing (or biting) can be a cat's reaction to a physical discomfort, such as kidney dysfunction, an old injury, or even arthritis. The primary stress target could also be cardiac related.

Your cat's veterinarian will decide which diagnostic tests (blood, biopsy, ultrasound, X rays) are needed to arrive at the correct diagnosis. Perhaps this information may throw some light on your cat's bizarre behavior. But even if it is a physical problem, generally, behavioral modifications are also necessary to quell his angst.

DIET

Many times the addition of a cat food with omega fatty acids 3 and 6, or supplements, such as a ¼ teaspoon brewer's yeast and ¼ teaspoon wheat germ in the food, or as tablets, provide the extra fat that helps to remedy the problem.

DISTRACTION

When your cat becomes excited, his outlet will be to overgroom and/or indiscriminately ingest. Before he starts to act out, distract him with affection or play. Continue this for at least a few minutes or he'll immediately revert to his fixation. Praise him, so your tone of voice and body language soothes his angst. Perhaps you might also try a stroll around the house.

How to address potential anxiety catalysts:

- Boredom—Your cat isn't a victim of the single-cat syndrome because he has a companion cat he adores. But maybe a cat-proof fish tank would strike his fancy or visits from a friend's dog perk him up. However, be careful in your selection of such a visitor so you don't overstimulate him. A floppy, low-key dog would fit the bill.

- Rivalry—Even though your cats have a great rapport, rivalry is always a part of the package. Remember to include each verbally when you address the other.

- Conflict—Life's daily needs may present a potential panic time. Make such times easier with a touch of simplicity. Provide your cats with individual feeding bowls and separate spots to eat to prevent conflict. The litter box should be kept in a quiet, safe area. Two scratching posts will avoid friction.

SEQUESTERED SANCTUARY

When you feel especially worried or exasperated, it's not unlikely that you might long to tuck yourself in bed or chill out in a luxurious bath. Whatever it is you long for, your objective is to feel safe and serene. When a cat is frightened or anxious, he often seeks a closet or bed as his security spot. Why not provide such a sanctuary for your cat so that he's protected when he's vulnerable? Such a sanctuary will provide a security spot for your cat and help to treat his anxiety, which manifests itself in overgrooming or indiscriminate eating. The more secure he feels, the less prone he is to act out. Such a sanctuary will inspire his confidence when he might feel threatened. Don't depend on him to know when he needs this protection. You will have to set up the guidelines. Coordinate his sequestered times with his high-anxiety times—when he's most prone to overgroom or ingest inappropriately.

The sanctuary should have all of his creature comforts. A large kennel or dog crate may be a suitable haven. Anticipate his anxiety times (feeding time, when there are visitors, when there is construction). Lead or carry him to his sanctuary at such times. This haven may also be a necessity when you're not home. A cat who has suffered previous separation anxiety is likely to feel discomfort when you're away. His sanctuary will protect him from any alien objects that he might ingest to quell his fears, and it will temper his need to mutilate himself. If necessary, an Elizabethan collar will provide additional protection.

His sanctuary may be a temporary measure or his home base. You might want to decorate it to inspire your own acceptance of this facility. If you fault yourself for this provision, he will be affected by your feelings. You are not trying to confine him to upset or punish him. This security object is the environment he needs to overcome and recover from his pervasive fear and dis-ease. Soft radio music and/or an audiotape may increase his serenity.

Don't be surprised if after a while he seeks the comfort of his sanctuary by choice. A cat eventually associates and accepts the source of good feelings. Gradually, you will help him to erase his feelings of fear so he doesn't have to resort to self-destructive behavior.

AUXILIARY RELIEF

Your cat may need a psychotropic (e.g., anti-anxiety) drug or a homeopathic remedy, Chinese herbs or the Bach flower remedies (see page 149) as an adjunct to his recovery program. As he recovers, his dosage can usually be decreased. Acupuncture, acupressure, and massage are also therapeutic measures.

The more you can give your cat in the form of a sensible program to overcome his dis-ease, the sooner he will put a stop to his abusive behavior.

Music Therapy as a Relaxation Technique

My late cat, Sunny-Blue, was the catalyst for my discovery of the therapeutic effect of music on feline behavior. He was a reformed attack cat who clearly benefited from the use of relaxation techniques to increase his tolerance of stress. One of his symptoms of anxiety was nocturnal hyperactivity. His piercing cries and leaps across my bed were a nightly routine. Then several years ago I listened to a cassette of a broadcast I had done for BBC radio, and Sunny relaxed as he listened with me. When the program ended, his tail flicked and his back rippled, signifying the return of his tension. But when I reran the cassette, he again curled up between the cassette player and me. His body relaxed as we listened to my voice on the tape. So I made Sunny his own personal tape, on which I frequently mentioned his name and the name of his companion, Ziggy Star-Dust. But it wasn't until I added the sounds of humpback whales, the ocean, seagulls, and a flute to the background that Sunny's response became truly remarkable. Within a week, his nocturnal rampaging was on the wane. Sunny's recovery formed the basis for the use of music therapy on audiocassettes in my practice.

Did you ever notice how sensitive your cat is to your moods? It's because he's affected by your tone of voice, your body language, and even by the way you breathe. When you are a bit over the edge, why not cushion your cat's reaction with music? Your cat may not have a particular problem that needs a private session from a cat behavior therapist, but a relaxation cassette makes an ideal security blanket for those times when your cat is under stress.

MAKE YOUR OWN AUDIOCASSETTE

You'll need:

1. An inexpensive audiocassette player-recorder; if you purchase one that has autoreverse, it will play back continuously (all day, if need be), providing continuous relaxation
2. A sixty-minute cassette (thirty minutes per side) is adequate
3. Your cat's (or cats') presence at a time when you're both (or all) in a mellow mood
4. Their favorite toys
5. Grooming comb or brush
6. Soft, uninterrupted music (I've had the greatest success with New Age music because it is among the lowest in tension)
7. Catnip (optional)

The recording session:

1. Choose a sunny, cozy spot where you can comfortably recline.

2. Indulge your cat with catnip in advance if it leaves him with a mellow feeling.

3. Tune in on happy thoughts, breathe freely, and turn on the recorder.

4. Talk about your cat's endless virtues and repeat his name frequently as you stroke him.

5. Include your favorite song or poem. Incorporate talk of good times you've shared and happy moments in your relationship.

6. To minimize your cat's fear of the sound of a telephone, crying baby, or barking dog, you can include these sounds so your cat will have a secure and positive association with them when they occur.

7. Address your cat by name again when you're ready to end your therapy session. This personal touch will stroke your cat's ego.

Turn on the cassette player before you leave home in the morning, or, if you are going away for a few days, instruct your cat sitter to start the cassette in the morning and turn it off at night. Remember, your cat can sense your anxiety long before it's manifested in your behavior. A relaxation cassette with music can ease the tension your cat may sense in you and pick up from you. Coincidentally, *you* may benefit as well!

Litter Box Problems

You just don't get it! Every cat you've ever had has been fastidious in his litter box habits. But your present cat is a problem. Sometimes he'll use the box religiously for days, and then suddenly he'll start to leave puddles and piles near the box, in the hallway, on the sofa, or sometimes on the bed.

INDISCRIMINATE URINATION, SPRAYING, AND DEFECATION

How to React to a Litter Box "Incident"

Your cat has had an incident, and you're terribly miffed. Sure, you understand why and what you should do. But what can you say so you'll release your frustration and not provoke him to do it again? You realize he's already upset and he'll eventually recover. Help!

You can express your feelings by saying, "Oh, no, you did it again!" You can even scream into a pillow. But it's important that he know you're on his side. So tell him he's getting better and that you're both doing your best. These words of encouragement will convey that you're there for him. You don't want to increase his anxiety level. True, he won't understand your words, but he'll sense you're a friend and not a foe.

Yes, you're rightfully confused and frustrated. But your cat shares your discomfort. His behavior is so bizarre in order to alert you to his physical and/or emotional dilemma. It's a formal protest. By avoiding the litter box, his message is conveyed in no uncertain terms. Your cat may be reacting to any of the following problems:

- Untidy litter box—Your cat's protest may be because of poor sanitation. Scoop the litter *daily* even if it's the clumping kind. Wash the entire box weekly. Perhaps a new box is in order.

- Type of box—A covered box suits many a cat, but your cat may not like to relieve himself in a tunnel-like space. Try him with an open box. If you have space, keep the covered box handy so he has a choice.

- Litter aversion—Your cat may object to the type of litter you decided to purchase because your friend's cat likes it and because you had a coupon that made it a real bargain. Don't ignore his rejection. It's *his* preference that counts. Toss the new brand out and return to his old faithful. I prefer organic litters such as Cat Country and Little Tiger because they are earth-friendly and flushable.

- Need for privacy—The box should be in a private but *accessible* spot. A kitten can become confused and disoriented easily. Escort him to the box and praise his performances.

- Toilet conflict—You almost had your cat trained to share your toilet, but he had second thoughts. He's decided to use the floor for his deposits and puddles. It's time to return his litter box. Evidently, he may not want to use a human toilet. Don't be stubborn, or his stress could activate a bladder problem.

PHYSICAL PROBLEMS THAT CAN LEAD TO POOR LITTER BOX BEHAVIOR

- Parasites—Your cat may be besieged by parasites such as those that cause coccidiosis, which is a common but difficult protozoa to isolate and identify. Giardia is another parasite that wreaks havoc with a cat's health. A fecal analysis is usually the first step to determine treatment.

- Chronic injury—Your cat may stand or lean over the box at toilet time, causing him to miss the box entirely. Pain from a past injury to the pelvis or adjoining area can be the source of discomfort. An X ray may be necessary to locate the problem. Arthritic pain may also be the culprit. Medication and possibly massage should ease this type of pain.

- Constipation—Dried segments of stool in and about the litter box could be a sign of constipation. Indiscriminate urination can accompany this ailment. Feed the cat a laxative gel, and/or a dab of butter or vegetable oil to help to soften the stool. There are also foods high in fiber and fiber supplements that your cat's veterinarian can recommend or prescribe. Massage and daily brushing will aid your cat's circulation and reduce tension, which contributes to constipation.

- Diarrhea—Unformed stools are common and are usually deposited anywhere but in the litter box. Diarrhea may be a result of ingestion of plants, a food allergy, an intestinal problem, parasites (see parasites, above), or a sudden change in diet. Consult your cat's veterinarian if diarrhea persists.

- Inflammatory bowel disease—Inflammatory bowel disease (IBD) is the most common chronic gastrointestinal disorder of cats. The small or large intestine becomes filled with cells that don't belong there and cause chronic diarrhea and/or vomiting. An endoscopy is usually needed to diagnose this condition.

- Impacted anal glands—The anal glands are on either side of the rectum, and excessive grooming in the anal area is frequently indicative of discomfort caused by impacted glands. A trip to the vet is usually necessary to have them checked and emptied. Relief should get your cat back on target.

- Bladder infection or bladder stones—A bladder infection is usually manifested by difficult urination and is generally arrested with medication, such as an antibiotic. Surgery is frequently the solution for stones, which are formed of minerals. Sometimes the stones can be dissolved by medication and diet.

- Kidney degeneration—The kidneys are organs in the abdominal cavity that remove metabolic waste products from the blood. When the kidneys degenerate, medication, restricted diet, and rehydration with fluids administered at home or at the veterinary hospital are the usual treatments. As with all of these problems of disfunctions, kidney failure or renal failure can cause a cat to urinate or defecate inappropriately or indiscriminately. Kidney failure is a major cause of death in older cats.

- Thyroid disorder—The thyroid gland regulates metabolism and body growth. Your cat's toilet habits can be affected by an over- or underactive thyroid. The treatment is either long-term medication or surgery.

- Respiratory difficulties—Asthma can trigger stress that may result in deviant litter box habits. Medication and/or a stress-reduction regimen should be effective. Asthma is often an allergic disorder, characterized by wheezing and difficulty breathing.

- Cardiac dysfunctions—Cardiomyopathy is the major type of heart disease diagnosed in the cat and is sometimes fatal. The disease takes two forms: dilated cardiomyopathy, which is enlargement of all the hearts' vessels, and lack of taurine, or hypertrophic cardiomyopathy, in which the muscle that forms the left ventricular wall becomes extremely thickened and unable to function. Medication can regulate cardiomyopathy in many instances if diagnosed in time. Cardiac problems can cause obvious discomfort in a cat's respiration. As with all of these disfunctions, litter box problems are a symptom or secondary effect of the primary problem (e.g. asthma, diabetes).

- Onset of sexual maturity—An intact cat will *often* avoid the box upon sexual maturity. Untidy toilet habits will usually cease about two weeks after surgery.

- Retained ovary, ovarian tissue, or testicle after surgery—These are reproductive organs that are removed when a cat is spayed or neutered. Such an occurrence is not common but far from unprecedented. Exploratory surgery can be performed to locate and remove the source of the problem.

- Feline leukemia, infectious peritonitis, and AIDS— The feline leukemia virus (FeLV) is a virus that affects the lymphatic system, suppressing immunity to disease. Feline infectious peritonitis (FIP) is usually a fatal viral disease that causes fluid accumulation in the abdomen, jaundice, and anemia. Feline immunodeficiency virus (FIV) weakens the immune system and eventually causes death. It's contagious to other cats but not to other animals or humans. When a cat is afflicted with any of these critical disorders, his bladder and/or rectum may become secondary stress targets. There may not be organic signs, but the discomfort from the primary disease can affect these areas. Medication, diet modification, and stress reduction techniques are appropriate types of relief. (Vaccinations for these disorders are continuously being perfected.)

- Diabetes—This is a disease caused by not enough insulin, the hormone that regulates the ability of the body to use sugar. Diabetes is usually regulated with injections of insulin and proper diet. It's not uncommon for a diabetic cat to have bouts of indiscriminate urination until his treatment program is regulated. A cat often manifests these bouts before a diagnosis of diabetes.

BIZARRE BATHROOM RITUALS

Bathtub

Your cat tinkles over the bathtub drain and leaves deposits in the middle of the tub. His physical checkup didn't reveal anything unusual. But you don't want your cat's signature in your tub!

Leaving an inch or so of water in the tub might convince your cat to use his box. If he resorts to other inappropriate areas, provide two litter boxes—one with litter and one nearly empty. He might have opted for the tub because he prefers a smooth surface.

Over the Edge

Why must your cat tinkle over the edge of his litter box?

He may be doing this because of discomfort from an old injury or because of present physical discomfort, such as that caused by a bladder infection, for example. But it may be because of his mood or preference. You could use a covered litter box or place a larger box underneath his current one to absorb the puddle. If he sprays the wall, a piece of newspaper in a vertical position will absorb the spray.

Newspaper

Suddenly your cat has decided to use newspapers and magazines for his toilet. You thought this was the case because you were a messy housekeeper. But now, despite your newly acquired neatness, he seeks out your reading material.

Your cat's choice may be associated with maternal nostalgia. The mother cat usually takes care of her kitten's wastes when she grooms them. Although paper does not resemble a mother cat's tongue, the paper, like the mother, is soft and cozy in texture.

A bout of anxiety may have caused him to resolve his nostalgia by seeking out a comfortable object. His new discovery may become a habit or may disappear when he feels secure. To curb this bad habit, fill his litter pan with strips of newspaper; a plastic liner is optional. Tissue paper or paper towels can also be used. Eventually, you can provide a second litter box filled with his favorite cat litter. If and when he uses this box exclusively, you can remove the box filled with newspaper. But don't try to rush his decision because it may add to his insecurity. Continue your neatness campaign so he isn't tempted to use other inappropriate areas or objects.

Bath Mat

Your cat will christen the bath mat if it's left on the floor, but otherwise he always uses his box. The bath mat may remind him of his soft and furry mom. Because it's comfy for you, it may also make it more attractive for him. Make it a rule to keep the bath mat out of his reach when not in use.

Products to Curb or Neutralize the Odor

A sweet-smelling shampoo will clean the area and remove the offensive scent. Nature's Miracle is an environmentally safe, biodegradable deodorizer that can be purchased at most pet supply shops. Neutron Industries in Cincinnati, Ohio (800-421-8481) also makes a citrus deodorizer. Evsco Pharmaceuticals has a spray deodorizer called the Equalizer Carpet Stain and Odor Eliminator that works on furniture, floors, and other areas. It can be purchased through veterinary hospitals.

Important Reminder

Rule out a medical problem with a checkup. *Never* assume your cat only has a behavioral problem. It may be solely a medical problem or a combination of both, and you will need behavioral and medical input to correct your cat's behavior. A physical problem can trigger an emotional dysfunction, and the latter can wreak medical havoc. For complete recovery, you must treat the entire cat.

ANXIETY AND LITTER BOX PROBLEMS

Your cat checks out A-OK medically, but he is still having litter box problems. He had a bladder problem years ago that the veterinarian treated with medication. There could be some undetected irritation that reappeared. Your cat responded to the new medication, but a few weeks later his toilet habits are delinquent. Now it's obvious you must have a program to make him feel better.

It's been a difficult year for the two of you. You started a new job a few months ago, moved to your present apartment last year, separated from your beau of five years, lost your dog to cancer, adopted a puppy whom your cat hated and who now lives with your former beau, and lost your mother. From what you've read, this spells out superseparation anxiety and culture shock. The bottom line is that you must have a practical program to correct your cat's behavior. You don't want to continue to resent him because you love him too much. There must be a way!

Behavioral Program

Yes, there is a way to help your cat, but don't despair if he doesn't mend his ways immediately. Chances are you may notice changes in other aspects of his behavior before his litter box habits become consistently acceptable. For instance, he may become less timid or aggressive.

His deviant toilet behavior is a symptom or a reflection of how he feels. Unfortunately, his other symptoms may respond more quickly to treatment than his indiscriminate toilet habits. When a cat deviates from his normal fastidious and cat-like elimination, it reflects the fact that he or she feels utterly powerless and has been distraught for quite a while before this behavior surfaced. However, you were probably not terribly bothered by whatever clues he did exhibit, so his discomfort escalated and his litter box problems got worse.

See pages 159 to 161, which explain how to rule out or correct an untidy litter box, an improper type of box, litter aversion, the need for privacy, or the startle effect.

You may notice that there are occasions when your cat may start to sniff around, look somewhat disoriented, run to the litter box, give a perplexed look, and finally choose to "litter" a spot other than the box. There are other times when his box will be his target. This behavior is a classic example of the angst your cat feels and is a form of an anxiety attack.

How to Relieve an Anxiety Attack or Desensitize Your Cat

When your cat has such an anxiety attack, speak softly to him and escort him to his litter box. If necessary, carry him, but remember to keep your body relaxed so you don't increase his tension. Continue to speak to him softly and praise him if he uses the box. Leave the room and close the door behind you if he conveys the feeling that he wants more privacy. You can open the door a crack if he feels pressured. If he uses the box, praise him and remove his deposit. It may turn out to be a false alarm, where he was clearly anxious, but his urge to use the litter box subsided. Despite this behavior, continue to escort and support him verbally when he exhibits his anxiety. This will calm and comfort him. Eventually, he may race you to his box with your words of praise as his reward. His rectum and/or bladder are his stress targets, and when he feels anxious, they become sensitized. He then deviates from his normal toilet habits to communicate his discomfort.

Here are some other steps to help the two of you to overcome his problem.

- Provide him with a second litter box that's lined with strips of newspaper. This may boost his morale and his sense of comfort.

- Soft music will calm the two of you. See Chapter 10 for more on relaxation techniques if you would like to make an audiotape to relax your cat. Massage is another way to relieve his body of tension, and brushing is a plus if he's receptive. The looser his body is, the better he feels.

- Help to reduce his angst by announcing your transitions, by saying, for example, "I have to make a phone call" or "I'm going into the bedroom." These words will keep him from becoming startled by your change of activity. Sequester him in a comfy area with his creature comforts if you know a particular guest, event, delivery, or construction work may rattle him.

- Reduce rivalry with a companion animal by mentioning his name when you interact with his companion. This will make him feel connected and in control.

- Diet contributes to his well-being. Good nutrition that is bladder sensitive enhances his resources.

Sequestering as a Means of Ending an Anxiety Attack

This technique should be used when the other tips aren't sufficient. To prevent incidents and provide your cat with a calm environment, you can sequester him at his high-anxiety times. If his incidents are in the morning, sequester him with his breakfast and litter pan. Do this gently so he doesn't feel he's being punished. This private time gives him the opportunity to go about his business without your morning transitional angst. Follow the same procedure if his panic time is in the evening when you return home. Sequester him with his dinner, etc., while you get settled. Sometimes it's necessary to use this technique whenever you're going to be away from home. It provides your cat with the security he needs if and when he feels anxious. It will become his haven if you treat it as one. Remember, he's sensitive to your feelings and you want him to truly feel that you're on his side.

Auxiliary Support: A Last-ditch Way to Relieve Anxiety

A tranquilizer, antipsychotic drugs, Chinese herbs, Bach flower remedies (or other homeopathic remedies) and/or acupuncture may be used to relieve your cat's angst. But it's the program of *reconstructive therapy* that will give him the ability to release the fear he feels and to incorporate new coping mechanisms so he can live a healthier and happier life.

MISCONCEPTIONS ABOUT LITTER BOX PROBLEMS

Fiction: My cat does this out of spite. He knows where his box is, yet doesn't use it to make me angry.

Fact: Your cat's incidents are an SOS. He purposely avoids the box to signal his distress, which may be medical, emotional, or a combination of the two.

Fiction: He'll never get better.

Fact: With the correct regimen and your understanding and patience, your cat can recover.

Fiction: If he recovers and has an "incident," it's back to square one.

Fact: No, a setback is not the end of recovery because he's been made stronger and will bounce back faster. Also, you know what to do to give him the help he needs.

Fiction: Incidents will come out of nowhere.

Fact: You'll be able to anticipate his vulnerable times. A change in environment, your personal life, or your work schedule or travel are common anxiety catalysts. Anticipate your cat's potential angst and give him the props you've used before to maintain his physical and emotional health. You might even want to schedule a therapy session for stress reduction.

Fiction: A new home would solve his problem.

Fact: A new home might help if his deviant behavior was the result of a tense relationship with a particular companion or person, or if he needed more attention, which the new home could provide. But if his problem remains unresolved, his misbehavior will probably surface whenever he feels threatened or vulnerable. So it would be best to at least start him on the road to recovery before you find him a new home.

"She's very possessive."

Travel

TRAVEL WITHOUT YOUR CAT

London's going to be lots of fun. It would be terrific to take your cats with you, but England has a six-month quarantine for animals. A friend of yours moved there recently, and she has four cats. She was very lucky because she knew of an exceptionally fine place for them to be quarantined. She visited them frequently, and they had their own little cubicle with their favorite toys. She even made a tape of herself talking to them with music playing in the background. The cats listened to their tape when she wasn't there and even sometimes when she visited them so the association was a very pleasant one. If you ever move to London, you'll get the name of that place or do some research so your cats have comfy accommodations. Perhaps the quarantine rule may be modified or even lifted by then. There may be a major change in that if you travel to England through another country, a quarantine will not apply. Check with the British Embassy or your travel agent or airline. It's very controversial in England. But for this trip, you'll travel without them. However, you wonder what would be best for them while you're away.

Boarding

Your cats should be boarded only if there are no other options. Visit the potential premises so you are certain that cleanliness, proper temperature, sunlight, and a competent staff are part of the package. Ideally, there should be a separate facility for cats.

If you do decide to board your cats, take along a couple of their favorite security objects, their food, and instructions on how they prefer to be handled. Don't forget to include the name of a friend they can contact in case of an emergency. Remember to leave instructions on any medication that may need to be administered and the name, address, and phone number of their vet. Finally, it would be terrific if someone that your cats liked could visit them a few times while you were away.

Cat Sitter

You may decide to engage a professional cat sitter to care for your cats if you don't have a friend or neighbor available. The cat sitter should make two daily visits. (See also Chapter 7.)

If you decide to have someone stay in your home, or if you take your cats to stay with a friend, you must be certain he or she is trustworthy. Unless your cats are extremely cat-friendly, try not to leave them with someone who has cats unless your cats can be kept in a separate area. You don't want to add to their stress level. You might want an overnight trial run to get an impression of how your cats will respond to the person. If this is inconvenient, at least have the person visit and interact with your cats before your trip.

TRAVEL WITH YOUR CAT

If you have a senior cat with a sensitive disposition and a chronic medical problem, he is not your best travel candidate. It might be best for him to be cared for in his own environment. Otherwise, there are many cats who travel well and even enjoy themselves.

Automobile

Sedation, either oral or by injection, may be needed if the trip is more than four hours. Consult your cats' veterinarian for the various options. You might want to give your cats a trial dosage of the sedative before your trip to make sure it will be effective. Dramamine might help if your cats have a quirky stomach. Take your cats for a short spin so they become acquainted with your car.

INSIDE THE CAR

Arrange the litter box in a convenient spot. Most cats travel best inside their carrier, because it is safe and snug. If your cats have free range, make sure the windows are open only a crack. A kitty harness might also be advisable. Traffic noises and wide-open spaces may disorient your cat. Soothe him and keep him away from the windows.

SHORT STOPS

Park in a shady spot if it's a warm day. Leave the windows open a crack if you're going to be gone for a while. A sunny 75 degrees may be equal to 120 degrees in a closed auto. Don't forget to lock your doors and tell your cats you'll be right back.

ENCOURAGE CALM ARRIVALS

Your cats may chatter a lot or hide when you reach your destination, or they may have a delayed reaction if they have been tranquilized. They should adapt to their new environment within a few days. But you should make their arrival a smooth one with the following instructions:

- Set up their litter box and water bowl in the bathroom (or in a small room).
- Bring their carrier(s) into the bathroom with you and close the door.
- Open the carrier(s) so your cats can become familiar with the litter box and bathroom.
- Leave the carrier(s) open so they have a security object with their scent they can retreat to.
- Stroke them, talk to them softly, and be generous with your hugs.
- After they're comfortable in the bathroom, they can explore new frontiers. But show them one room at a time if your place is large. You don't want them to become overwhelmed by a strange and vast new space. Offer them a pinch of catnip.
- A dab of butter on their paws will distract them if they're overanxious. They'll forget to feel upset as they lick away at the butter.

Transition

It may take your cats a few days to adapt to their new environment, and they may even hide until they feel braver. If this behavior lasts for more than a few days and their appetite and toilet habits become abnormal, contact a nearby veterinarian. Emotional stress can trigger a medical problem.

Outdoor Privileges

If you're determined that your cats should venture outdoors, there are precautions you should take to ensure their safety.

They should be totally familiar and comfortable with their indoor environment before they are allowed outdoors. Provide them with a collar and identification even if they are tattooed. A flea collar or medallion may also be needed if they haven't received oral medication for flea prevention.

Install a commercial kitty door if possible, but acquaint them with it before their outdoor foray. Accompany them on their first short strolls around the house. A kitty harness and leash would also be helpful. Your cats should become familiar with the immediate area while under your supervision. This will acquaint them with where to hide or how quickly they can return inside if they have a panic attack. Lure them home before sundown with dinner. They should be inside at night.

Hotel Hopping

There are many hotels that are cat-friendly. The Ritz-Carlton and Four Seasons hotels are especially so. Gaines dog food puts out a booklet called "Traveling with Towser" that lists hotels and motels where dogs are welcomed. Cats are usually permitted if dogs are. It's not uncommon for the hotel or motel to ask you to sign an agreement holding you responsible for any damage your cats may cause.

ARRIVAL AT THE HOTEL

Make certain your cats' carriers are easily identifiable. If your cats start to cry, talk to them softly. The less excited you are, the less vocal they'll be. For more instructions, see page 176.

The Do Not Disturb sign should be put on your door whenever you leave your room. You don't want someone to enter your room and accidentally let your cats out. Inform your maid that your cats are with you and instruct her not to leave your door ajar at any time.

DEPARTURE

Your room should be spic-and-span for the next person who stays in your room.

Travel to Another State or Foreign Country

Various vaccinations are usually required before entry. Consult your cats' vet for information on domestic and foreign requirements, including any quarantines. You can also contact the embassy of any foreign country for information regarding your cats' entry.

QUARANTINES

England has a six-month quarantine (see pages 173–174), and Hawaii has recently reduced its quarantine from three months to one month. There may be some islands of the Caribbean where cats are not permitted. Check with the particular island's embassy for more information.

TRAVEL BY AIR

Check with your airline on their requirements for animal carriers. Acquaint your cats with their carrier a few weeks before your trip and refer to the tips mentioned earlier in this chapter.

ADVANCE RESERVATION

Generally, only two companion animals are allowed in the cabin with you, so be sure to make your reservation far in advance. Sometimes a particular airline will allow two cats to travel in the same carrier if it fits comfortably under the seat in front of you. Request seat assignments for your entire trip so you are sure to have a place for your cats. If you want to take more than two cats, they probably won't be allowed. Check with the particular airline.

HEALTH CERTIFICATE

Your cats should have a medical examination within ten days of travel so you can present their health certificate from the veterinarian to the airline. Your cats will need the appropriate vaccinations, and the certificate will indicate that they are free of any infectious disease.

IDENTIFICATION

The carrier should be labeled with your name, home address, phone number, and information about your destination. Keep their health certificates with your airline ticket, and you might want to include your cats' photos.

There are companies that provide special auto transportation for your cats to the airport if they have to travel in cargo and you have to leave before they do.

ARRIVAL AT THE AIRPORT

Don't allow your cats to be put through the X-ray machine. Breathe freely and think "relax." Try to sit in a quiet area while you wait for the plane.

IN FLIGHT

Talk to your cats softly. Wait to deplane after most of the other passengers.

CATS IN CARGO

- Avoid extremely hot or cold weather.
- Call the airlines for requirements for cats as cargo.
- Try to travel when you know planes will not be crowded.
- Your cats should not fly in the cargo hold if they have any respiratory problems.
- A short-faced breed of cat, such as a Persian, is especially vulnerable to breath deprivation and heat strokes.
- Inform the flight attendant and captain that your cats are in cargo.

ARRIVAL

Stroke and talk to your cats to make sure they're aware of your presence. Ask an airline employee to bring your cats to you so they are not put on a loading dock or in a concrete waiting room in inclement weather. When you arrive at your final destination, refer to tips earlier in this chapter.

Travel by Railroad, Bus, or Boat

Some railroads permit cats on board, and you can place their carrier on your lap or beside you on your seat. Your cats' carrier should be sturdy and well ventilated. If your cats travel in the baggage car, the railroad's personnel will usually give your cats water at station stops along the way.

You are usually allowed time to visit and tend your cats at station stops that last ten or more minutes.

Many major interstate bus companies in the United States don't permit cats. The same applies to some intracity lines, where it will usually depend on the whim of a particular bus driver. A smile and a polite demeanor may gain your cats entrance.

Most cruise ships are not cat-friendly. But there are some that have kennels. Check with the particular liner for specific information.

Camping

Generally, an outdoor cat adapts best to camping. Camping is a special interest with people and probably all the more so with the feline species. If you decide to take your cat on a camping trip, a kitty harness and leash is mandatory, and you should refer to page 175 for supplies and other information. Outdoor Jaunts for Indoor Cats, on pages 43–44, will also give you related tips.

Medical Conditions and Travel

If your cat has a medical problem, the stress of travel may exacerbate it. Discuss this with your cat's veterinarian. A tranquilizer may relieve your cat's emotional stress.

Returning Home

You shouldn't be astonished if your cats are disoriented after your return home. Let them settle in slowly. Some soft music may ease their transition. Frequent travel with your cats will increase their tolerance of the culture shock. You may even decide to travel together around the world!

Your Cat and Changing Human Relationships

INTRODUCING A NEW PERSON TO YOUR CAT

You and your cats have always been the perfect trio. Many people have played minor roles in your household for short periods of time, but your present "interest" is going to be a permanent fixture. So far your cats don't seem to mind, but you want to take every precaution you can to make sure there's no resentment. You'll do anything you can so your relationship with your cats isn't damaged.

Before the Move

The following pointers will help you keep your cats from feeling threatened by the newcomer:

- Try to have some of your cats' meals coincide with this person's visits so they will associate the person's presence with something pleasant.

- Give your cat gifts during these visits.

- Never force them together. Cats prefer to choose their friends.

- Try always to include the cats' names in your conversations with this person so the cats feel included and cared about. If they start to feel rejected, they'll withdraw and resort to fight or flight.

- Keep an article of clothing from the person on your bed to familiarize your cats with his or her scent. Even if they didn't sleep with you before, they may decide to bed down with you because of the newcomer. The grass is always tastier when there's competition. You clearly don't want your bed to be a war zone, so give the cats time to adjust to a newcomer.

Move-in Day

This should be a low-key kind of day. Try to spend most of your time at home. You want your cats to think of your chosen person as an additional source of love and attention—not a competitor for your affection.

Getting Adjusted

Your cats should gradually accept the new resident. Remember to stay relaxed and have confidence that they will bond happily. If you are a one-cat person, a second cat may ease the pressure of a triangular relationship (you, the newcomer, and your cat) or may ease your cat if he is very upset about the change in balance of power in the house.

See Chapter 8 for how to select and introduce a new companion cat or kitten.

INTRODUCING A NEW PERSON WITH CATS

Before the Arrival

Your future roommate should visit a few times, but don't allow him or her to interact with your cats too much. Otherwise, they may feel betrayed when the roommate moves in with *additional* cats. Present your cats with the new cats' toys so that they are familiarized with the new cats' scent. The cats should all be neutered, spayed, and checked out medically at least two weeks before the introduction.

Arrival Day

- Feed your cats a light meal before or at the time of arrival. This will help them associate the newcomer with something pleasant.

- Keep your roommate's cats in a neutral area apart from your cats for the first several days. If your roommate has a separate bedroom, it would be an ideal place for his or her cats. Your roommate should place his or her cats in their designated area and close the door.

- After a while, take their empty carrier to your cats. They can explore the interior and get a good whiff of the newcomers.

- Return the carrier to the newcomers so they can become familiar with your cats' scent.

- *Don't enter* the newcomers' space. You don't want to make your cats jealous. Dote on your cats while your roommate concentrates on his or hers so the boundaries are defined. Your cats must feel that you are theirs and that your roommate is connected to his or her cats. If you try to play round robin with your attention, the boundaries will become blurred. This will instigate trouble!

- Attach a screen door (unless there are glass panes in the present door) or stack half screens and fasten the screens with self-sticking Velcro on the door frame so the cats can see but not touch each other. Your cats will probably congregate outside the newcomers' door. This will help them to acclimate to each other's scent. Within a week or so, hisses should diminish and their tolerance for each other should begin to grow. You can now switch areas so they can check out each other's terrain. The door should be closed between them so they remain separate. Repeat this technique for about a week.

Introduction Day

Within two weeks a meeting should be able to take place. Select a quiet day. You and your roommate should be comfortable and relaxed. Place food for each pair of cats in each territory so they will find it when they have their jaunt. Don't monitor their actions or they will react to your tension. Don't make overtures toward the newcomers, and your roommate should focus on his or her cats. If bickering becomes significant, use a spritz of water from a plant sprayer or scoot the cats back to their respective areas. But remember that there will have to be some aggressive interplay to establish roles. Your cats may be more aggressive than they were when they were the only cats in residence.

If the interactions are smooth, repeat the meetings for several days and finally leave the doors ajar. But continue to feed and care for the cats in their individual areas. Gradually, you may be able to establish communal areas. However, if the cats continue to hiss when they meet, repeat the procedure for the next couple of weeks. When they finally have worked out a tolerable living arrangement, you can leave the doors ajar for them to mingle. The time frame for them to adapt to each other will depend upon their confidence and experience. If necessary, you may need to tranquilize them for a while to relieve their fear.

Conclusion

Your responsibility is to your own cats. Remember that the newcomers are a threat to their territory and comfort. Your cats won't relax until they feel less vulnerable. The more secure they feel, the more receptive they will be to the newcomers. So devote your attention to your cats. If you try to make the newcomers feel better by petting them, your cats will resent you and distance themselves even more from the newcomers. Just remember, your roommate is there for them, and you must be there exclusively for your cats.

CATS AND KIDS

Newborns

Until now you've always thought of your cat as your baby. But now there's a slight wrinkle. A newborn baby is soon to enter your life. Will your cat resent this colossal change? How can you prevent any avoidable chaos?

PRENATAL PREPARATION

Your well-meaning relatives warn you to declaw your cat to safeguard your new baby. Don't even dream of such a mutilation! Without his claws, your cat will be more apt to feel insecure and threatened. Consequently, he'll bite. Keep his claws trimmed, but when he feels threatened by the baby's cries or movements, he'll be more likely to retreat than to seek baby out.

The energy level of a baby is usually very high. A baby moves abruptly and makes lots of noise. These can disconcert a cat who's been used to a quiet environment. It's best to sequester your cat in a separate room from your baby when he or she is crying or noisy. If your cat is intact, have him neutered before the baby's arrival because a tomcat's energy level can be very high at times, and intact toms are far more likely to become aggressive. He may even spray the baby's belongings and assume an aggressive posture toward your child. Female cats should also be spayed.

Specific tips:

- Try to include your cat's name in conversation when you speak of baby so he feels included and not excluded.

- Sprinkle some baby powder or baby oil on your skin or robe so your cat becomes familiar with the baby's scent.

- Prepare a high perch for your cat to chill out on whenever the baby's decibel level becomes intolerable.

- Allow him to sniff the baby's furniture and other belongings so your cat's curiosity is satisfied.

- Have plenty of his favorite foods and treats on hand when baby arrives.

- Make an audiotape of a crying baby and play the tape frequently so your cat becomes familiarized with the new sound. Stroke and talk softly to him as the tape plays to form a positive association.

- If you hire an au pair, try to find one who favors cats so yours won't be neglected.

- Arrange to have a neighbor's child come in and spend time with your cat the day of baby's arrival. When possible, continued visits will make your cats feel doted on.

- If you're a single parent, a cat-friendly helper is especially invaluable.

Baby's Arrival

Try to arrange to have your cat fed shortly before baby's arrival to create a positive association. Permit him to smell some of baby's belongings to acquaint him with the baby's scent. Remember to include your cat's name in your conversation as you interact with baby. This subtle mention will prevent him from feeling rejected and anxious. Whenever you leave the room with baby, verbalize your actions in a short sentence to avoid transitional angst. Otherwise your cat may become suspicious and resentful. If this reaction intensifies, he may become very stressed and his behavior will mirror his angst.

Put a screen or netting over your baby's crib until the baby is old enough to move and roll over if you don't want your cat to crawl into baby's crib. (Usually a window screen can be placed over a bassinet.) You can also have an intercom that will allow you to hear baby's cries and monitor any sounds when you are in another room. Such a device will enable you to close the door to baby's room if you don't want the cat to enter. You might want to install a temporary screen door so your cat can look but not get in.

BREASTFEEDING

Don't be surprised if your cat stretches out nearby you and baby if you breastfeed. He'll be affected by the happy, fulfilling feelings that nursing creates.

FELINE MEDICAL PROBLEMS

Sometimes the arrival of a baby can cause a cat to have medical problems. The baby's high energy level may trigger bladder, skin, or respiratory problems in a sensitive, thin-skinned cat. If such a cat doesn't respond well to medication, a new home where the cat is the center of attention may be the best solution. But most cat-versus-baby problems can be readily solved if the people have the time and energy to work them out.

IMPROVED CATSONALITY

Because your cat has always been somewhat aloof, you wonder how he'll be affected by your new baby. He may become so fascinated and intrigued with baby that he seeks out baby's company. A baby's energy can sometimes relax a cat and bring out his protective instincts.

FELINE NANNY

If your cat is baby shy he will probably keep a safe distance from baby. But don't be surprised if he acts as surrogate nanny and alerts you when your baby needs you—before you're even aware of it. A cat's superior sensitivity makes this a common occurrence.

Introduction of Children

Your cat could experience severe culture shock with the arrival of a child into the household—especially if children are alien to him. It's best to prevent undue stress with preventive care. Try to arrange to have some cat-friendly children visit before the "new addition" so your cat isn't totally surprised. During such visits the children shouldn't approach your cat and should engage in low-key activities. Don't invite more than two children at a time.

You may choose to follow these suggestions:

- Allow your cat to become acquainted with a child's energy at a distance. This will establish trust.

- Allow the children to interact with your cat if your cat seeks them out.

- Double up on the attention you give your cat before and after the child arrives.

- Instruct the child on how to interact with your cat. Your cat should approach the child for attention, rather than to have the child seek him out.

- Keep your cat separate when the child has playmates over. Your want to avoid undue stress. Once he's bonded with the child, you can rethink the best option for when there are additional children in the house. Your cat should adapt to their presence gradually—if at all.

- Let the child feed the cat (if the child is old enough).

Don't overwhelm your cat with the child's presence. Time and patience will enable them to slowly bond. As your cat realizes the child is friend not foe, he will become receptive.

Fact or Fiction About Cats and Children

Fiction: A cat can suck the baby's breath.
Fact: Cats don't suck your breath. A cat could suffocate

a baby only if he slept across the baby's face and the baby was too young to move or roll out of the way.

Fiction: A pregnant woman will catch toxoplasmosis from her cat.

Fact: Anyone can contract this disease, although there are people who are naturally immune. It is caused by a microscopic-sized organism called *Toxoplasma gondii*. The infective organism is found in cat feces, but it is also common in uncooked beef and other sources. Symptoms include a sore throat and possibly swollen lymph glands in the neck.

The danger is if the mother contracts the disease during the first three months of her pregnancy, as the organism can produce cysts in the brain of the fetus, which can cause mental retardation. To prevent this, she should not clean the litter box or, if she does, she should wash her hands thoroughly afterward.

Fiction: A cat is a source of infectious diseases to a baby.

Fact: The chance is greater that people will transmit diseases to the baby.

Fiction: A baby will contract ringworm from a cat.

Fact: Ringworm is a potential problem only if your cat shows signs of infection himself. If so, have your cat treated by a veterinarian and wash your hands thoroughly after handling your cat. You will all benefit if your baby's physician is cat-friendly so his solution isn't to abandon your cat.

Fiction: A cat will take possession of the baby's crib.

Fact: Your cat is apt to crawl into baby's crib when it's empty. The baby's scent intrigues him, as does the security of a closed-in, cozy spot. He wants to share the attention that the baby receives when in the crib. Cat-proof your baby's crib with a fabric dome or put a screen over the crib if you don't want your cat in the crib.

Fiction: There's no way to deter a child from mishandling a cat.

Fact: When your baby mishandles your cat, tell baby why this is a no-no. Rescue the cat if he can't get away himself. Show your child how to gently stroke the cat by holding his hand and using it to pet the cat. Be sure to watch them both while they're together.

INTRODUCING YOUR CAT TO PEOPLE ALLERGIC TO OR AFRAID OF CATS

You never dreamed you would fall in love with someone who's allergic to cats and an ailurophobe (someone who's afraid of cats) besides. There's no way you'd ever part with your cats. But what can be done so the three of you can live happily ever after?

Spay or Neuter Your Cats

Studies have shown that a person allergic to cats does better with a spayed female cat than an intact male because of the cat's high testosterone level. The risk is lower with a neutered male.

De-fur Your Home

People are allergic to substances found in cat saliva (on their fur and skin), so the more you can do to decrease the amount of shed hair, the more comfortable your intended will be.

- Air cleaners can be put throughout the house and there's a wide variety to choose from.*

- There are products to rub on your cats that will neutralize effects of their saliva and dander.

- If possible, choose area rugs and chairs and sofas with a minimum of padded upholstered surfaces. These can be steam cleaned more frequently and retain less cat dander.

- There are special antiallergy cleaning products that you can use on your carpets, special filters for your vacuum cleaner (Hepa filters; see below), and a water-operated vacuum cleaner that will help minimize the spread of dander. The Hepa air filtering vacuum is another option. You can contact Hammacher Schlemmer at 800-543-3366 for more information.

- Brush or comb your cats frequently. There are products you can use on their coat and supplements you can put in their food for shed reduction.

- Ask your cats' veterinarian if it would be safe to add an animal tranquilizer called acepromazine to their water. This is supposed to reduce the allergenicity of cat saliva and has worked for many cats. It's been effective in many situations, but may not be healthy for all cats. The cat's person should check with a veterinarian.

- Air conditioners and humidifiers can be effective. Ozone generators are risky because they can increase toxic gases.

- Wash or bathe your cat weekly and add Downy to the bathwater.

*You can consult the American Lung Association (800-586-4872) and request their "Residential Air Cleaning Devices Report" or visit the website of the Environmental Protection Agency (www.epa.gov) for more information. The Association of Home Appliance Manufacturers at 312-984-5800 tests air cleaners.

- If your home is spacious, set aside a room that is off limits to your cats where your intended can retreat when needed.

Medication

An over-the-counter antihistamine may control allergic reactions. But sometimes a prescription medication, such as Claritin, is needed. There is also a series of injections given by an allergist, which is frequently effective for allergic reactions to cats.

A vaccine that's under investigation may help future cat-allergy sufferers. Consult a cat-friendly allergist about this vaccine to see if it has been approved and accepted and/or if there is a new discovery.

A therapist may be helpful if the allergy is psychologically rooted. Behavior modification is especially beneficial to a person who is ailurophobic.

Alternative Therapy

A psychologically rooted allergy can often be treated with acupuncture, hypnotherapy, massage, and homeopathy. These methods can also be used if the allergic reaction is physical.

Asthma

Asthma can usually be treated with an inhaler. But if it's a severe condition, it may become critical if the cats are not kept in their own private sanctuary. This should be a last resort. Sometimes a chiropractor can help.

After the Move

Don't try to force your cats on your significant other or insist that he or she must interact with them. Sometimes cats will instinctively gravitate to an allergic or ailurophobic person, either to try to befriend them or because they're attracted by the person's anxious energy. Most cats are inclined to distance themselves from those who aren't friendly. If the cats lose their bedroom privileges, make it a point to sleep part of the night or morning with them. Loss of such special "time" can trigger severe separation anxiety and ultimately deviant behavior.

A Will Creates a Way

It's not uncommon for people to build up an immunity to a cat's presence out of sheer persistence.

Socialization of the Feral Cat

What to do? You wonder now if you really did the best thing for this cat. He's now stashed away in a very large kennel in a corner of your living room. Luckily, he's next to a sunny window and you can privatize his area with a large bamboo screen when necessary—but he's a feral cat. The stray cat appeared in your yard several months ago, and you became his meal ticket. He didn't miss a meal and his presence grew on you. But three weeks ago you noticed he was dragging his left hind leg. His facial expression was more agitated than his usual feral look—he looked in pain. You decided you must take action, so you borrowed a Have a Heart trap from the local rescue group, filled it with his favorite food, and left it in your yard that evening. If he was hungry, this was his only option.

The next morning you found him inside the trap and whisked him off to the vet. His injury was minor. Several days later, after tests and vaccinations, he was neutered, hospitalized for a few more days, and released to your care with a clean bill of health.

Now you wonder if you should return him to the great outdoors or socialize him so he can continue his life as a domesticated cat—your cat! The latter would be a great responsibility and a tremendous commitment. What do you do?

REALITY CHECK ABOUT SOCIALIZATION

Now that he is neutered, he can't impregnate a female and add to the overpopulation of homeless cats. He will still be able to retain his independence and vagabond lifestyle. When you can't provide food for him, you can arrange for a neighbor or rescue group to provide for him. Otherwise, you can slowly wean him from his daily feeding schedule so he will be motivated to seek food elsewhere. Because you don't tame or socialize him, he will be capable of fending for himself.

But if you decide to domesticate the stray cat you should feel committed to do the best you can for his advancement. Once he is relatively socialized, you should find him another home *if* your situation fails to provide him with the love and care he needs. Remember, if you tame a cat, he is totally dependent on your judgment and reliability—especially if he's an indoor cat. But even an outdoor cat is greatly affected by his relationship to his person. If you are quite sure that you can invest the time and patience it requires to socialize a feral cat, there are guidelines to follow that will ease some of the difficulties involved with this major transition.

PROVIDING FOR A FERAL CAT

If his kennel—or shall we say security object or sanctuary—is large enough, his food and water should be kept on a tray that you can remove easily. You may have to wear gloves if this movement frightens him and causes him to bat at your hands. His litter box should also be kept in a spot where it is convenient for you to remove. It might be necessary to use newspaper as litter if he scatters the cat litter with abandon. Finally, a washable cushion or towel should help to keep him cozy in his kennel.

Remember to talk to him softly whenever you interact with him or "his" belongings so he isn't taken by surprise. A feral cat is always on guard because to survive in the wild, he has to be defensive. To be taken unaware on the streets could have meant death. Keep your movements around him slow but steady. The more relaxed and composed you are, the calmer he'll be. A feral cat is exquisitely sensitive to your body language and tone of voice. It's this sensitivity that kept him aware of danger. He had to be suspicious so he could resort to fight or flight in time to save himself.

RELAXATION THERAPY

Because a feral cat must always be alert in order to survive on the streets, his whole being is tense. Relaxation can be critical to his adjustment to your home and his domestication. That is why the more techniques you can use to change his body posture and mind-set to a relaxed state, the easier his transition will be. Music therapy can increase relaxation, and Chapter 10 gives you the way to relax your cat using a mix of your voice and music on audiotape. Soft radio or CD music is another device, but it is not as effective. Massage, aromatherapy, aerobic exercise and dance are also terrific for stress reduction.

Your participation in any of these pursuits will give him vicarious relief. If you play a musical instrument, this is another form of therapy for him. It's important that you appreciate the music so your appreciation will be transferred to your cat. Conversely, if you aren't pleased, your cat will sense your unhappiness. Finally, if your cat is staying in a dog's kennel you might want to slip a cover over his quarters to protect him from any activities or actions that may startle him.

Don't expect him to accept everything the first time around. With a feral cat, it's the repetition of a particular activity that wins acceptance. After all, his mother taught him to be wary of anything *new or unexpected!* As a kitten, change represented danger, and consistency was the key. Anything new had to be inspected very slowly or avoided.

A feral cat especially is a creature of habit. His life depends on this. Change is initiated only when he chooses it—or there appears to be no other way. A feral's trust is *earned*—not given away!

VISITORS

When you have company, turn on a tape or soft music to help take his mind off the intrusion. If he stays in a dog's kennel, you might even drape a cover over his quarters so he doesn't feel threatened. Your cat will be less startled by low-key and gentle visitors. Don't encourage your company to approach him. The more protective you are of his space, the more confident he will become. It's most important that he develop this sense of composure and trust in his security spot or sanctuary. As he grows stronger, he will be able to cope with more intrusions. But you must remember to build his foundation of new growth slowly so it doesn't tumble apart. Don't be disillusioned if he has setbacks. As he becomes more self-assured, he will rebound more quickly.

MEDICATION

If you have to medicate him, conceal the medication in a small morsel of tasty food or gel. It's best to do so when he's most hungry. Pharmacists can now compound medication with a fishy or meaty flavor to counteract a bitter taste.

PHYSICAL CONTACT

When you feel he has settled into a comfortable routine and he doesn't shy away when you approach him, you can attempt to stroke his back while he eats. At this time his concentration will be on food and not on your contact. It will be a positive association. If he accepts this, be brief the first few times. You want to stop before he becomes fearful. Remember to keep your breathing and body relaxed, and you can wear gloves. It's best to be in a seated or outstretched position so you are at ease. He might prefer you to stroke his head. The type of contact will be determined by his preference.

After he becomes comfortable with your touch during meals, you can attempt to stroke him when he appears relaxed at other times. He's apt to be most receptive when he's sprawled out in a relaxed position and his breathing is even. If he accepts this contact, a few strokes will do it. Again, you want to stop before he loses his cool.

TRANSITIONS

Verbalize your change of action or motion so he isn't taken by surprise and made anxious. Say, "I have to answer the phone," "I'm going to the kitchen," "Someone's at the door." These comforting words will provide a segue to your next activity without startling him.

SEDATION

If you find that he is totally terrified by his new environment, and two or three weeks have passed without improvement, you might want to consider an antianxiety drug, such as Valium. Because Valium relaxes the skeletal muscles, it is the ideal drug to release his conditioned fear. Have the veterinarian do a blood test to decide if your cat is a safe candidate for Valium or another substance before starting treatment. I prefer to use brand names such as Valium, because the quality control with generic drugs isn't always accurate.

The selected sedation can be added to his food. It's usually more palatable if it's ground into a fine powder and mixed into a small morsel of tasty food. Although a drug, such as Valium, can cause temporary lack of coordination, because your cat is in a small space this effect won't cause any accidents. If the drug is effective, it should be given long term. As he becomes more confident and social, his dosage can be reduced slowly and eventually stopped when your cat is relatively comfortable with his new role. The right drug can definitely speed the socialization process.

Homeopathic Remedies

There are also homeopathic remedies that can hasten his progress, and these, too, can usually be concealed in his food. A remedy for fear should be included in his regimen. You can consult a homeopathic veterinarian or other knowledgeable source.

EXERCISE

Your new cat will eventually need to exercise. Although his sanctuary provides the security he needs, it lacks the space he needs to keep limber. After you've established a routine with him, you can prepare for his outings. Cat proof the room so he can't disappear under any furniture where you can't lure him out. Generally, a feral cat will stick close to the ground and won't be eager to explore tabletops, etc. This is because he feels more protected on the ground.

His first few outings should take place at a quiet time shortly before his next meal so he will be inclined to return to his sanctuary when his food arrives. Remove yourself from his path of entry so he has quick and easy access. If he appears hesitant, leave the room for a while so he can feel secure enough to return. However, return and secure the door to his sanctuary.

After he becomes comfortable with these outings, you can increase the amount of time he has to wander about. But don't give him access to other rooms because it might trigger culture shock. You want him to feel secure in his environment. Too much change too quickly could be stressful. Ideally, a small, sunny room provides the most adequate sanctuary for him, and he can be transferred to this room in his kennel. After he is settled in this new room, you can leave the door to his kennel ajar so he can venture out when he wishes. Remember to keep the door to this room closed and announce your arrivals and departures so you don't startle him. Finally, don't even think of moving his kennel because it is his primary security spot.

Play

You wonder why your new cat doesn't know how to play. He doesn't appear to react to the catnip you offer him and he seems to avoid the toys. He doesn't have a clue what to do with them!

His seriousness stems from his feral kittenhood, which was not about *play* but *existence.* Chances are his mother was always on the alert and this trait was learned by her kittens. But as time goes by and he becomes more secure he may begin to be affected by the catnip, which usually has a stimulating followed by a relaxing effect. This reaction may give him courage and an incentive to play. Dangle a string and be subtle and seductive so he will be enticed. Assume a sitting or reclining position so your body will be at ease. If he shows interest, repeat this a few times each day. A sturdy scratching post such as the Felix model from Seattle, Washington (206-547-0042) should capture his interest. Those on the East Coast can try the Karate Kat Post from Elmsford, New York (800-822-6628). Couple it with either company's scratch board, which provides a horizontal workout.

ROLE MODELS FOR FERAL CATS

You've never had two cats, but the other day you noticed how much fun your friend's two cats had together. One cat was clearly the mentor and caretaker of the other. Perhaps your feral cat would do well with such a role model. But you're not sure that you want to have two cats. There are many moments when you wonder why you became committed to *one.*

How to Choose the Second Cat

A companion may be the best solution to your cat's progress in his new way of life. As your cat observes your relationship with the newcomer, he may be inspired to follow his lead. He will learn that you don't harm the newcomer—in fact, you even nurture him. As his trust develops, he will slowly lose some of his learned and instinctual fear. The right role model should enable him to accept domesticity sooner.

An ideal companion may be a three- to four-month-old, healthy male or female kitten who's very playful and cat-oriented. The last trait is most important because you want a kitten who will amuse and stimulate your cat. If the kitten is more interested in people, your cat will play second fiddle. Although you want the kitten to be people-friendly, their being cat-friendly is the priority.

An adolescent neutered male or spayed female with the same qualities would also be appropriate. If you'd prefer to adopt an even older cat, he or she should also possess the same qualities. This particular candidate would be especially suitable if he or she had shared a loving and playful relationship with a male cat who was somewhat shy of people and preferred to take a supporting role. Such familiarity would help to ignite the new relationship.

Perhaps you are wary of committing to another cat. You could arrange to foster a cat for a local rescue group. You may even decide to keep it. Whichever candidate you decide on, make certain that he or she has been checked out medically—vaccinated and tested for leukemia and any other potential health threats. Try to match your cat with one of a similar color. A cat can distinguish color by scent, and familiarity would breed favor unless your cat has had an unpleasant experience with a cat of similar coloring.

Introducing the Companion

Because your cat is feral, he won't be as obsessed with your attention as a socialized cat usually is. That is why the introduction doesn't have to be as formal as it would be if your cat were socialized. Your interactions with the newcomer don't have to be limited.

When you bring the newcomer home, your cat should be in his kennel or security spot with its door closed. Try to arrange for an acquaintance to escort the newcomer in, and place the open carrier on the opposite side of the room from your cat. As you communicate with your cat, the escort can open the carrier so the newcomer can emerge at will. The escort should exit at this time so your cat isn't threatened by another person. Make sure the newcomer has access to the area where you have the litter box set up, and food and water should be available for him.

Continue to interact with your cat for a short while, but go out soon for a short jaunt. When you return, you can check out the new relationship. If the two appear to break bread together acceptably, you can open the door to your cat's shelter. Otherwise, encourage the newcomer to leave the room before letting your cat have his liberty. Repeat this process several times until you feel that the two can hang out with minimal upset. There may be instant acceptance of each other or it may take several days for them to click. Feline chemistry will play a major part in how quickly they bond. Once they do, however, don't be surprised if you suddenly find the two ensconced in your cat's kennel in a comfy and chummy way.

Devote energy to interacting with the newcomer so as to give your cat a good model of a cat-human relationship. The newcomer's reactions will be very different from the feral's reactions, which he received from his feral mother. When he and the newcomer truly become an "item," your cat will probably need to spend less and less time in his security spot. But continue to keep the door open for the times he does wish to retreat there. If he routinely uses the newcomer's box and prefers to eat with the newcomer, you can provide a smaller kennel or security box. Place it next to his original one for at least several days before you remove his original sanctuary. He may always need some sort of hideaway.

TIME FRAME FOR SOCIALIZATION

You wonder how long it will take to socialize your feral cat. Will it take forever if he doesn't have a feline role model? How social will be become?

Socialization usually moves faster if there is a feline role model present. A cat-friendly dog may also offer inspiration and courage to trust. The process will take longer without such a role model. The length of time also depends on how fearful your cat is. But as he becomes confident and reaches out to you, his encouragement will inspire you, and you won't count the days. Remember, each day is a testament to his new way of life, and each day he will become stronger emotionally. Even if he appears to have regressed for one day or two, don't worry; this will pass and he'll continue to forge ahead.

How extroverted and affectionate he'll eventually become depends on his individual catsonality. Like that of any other cat, his catsonality is the sum of qualities he has inherited from his parents, plus his ability to express them and his own experience. Remember that even cats with socialized parents who have been nurtured by people since kittenhood are not always extroverted and affectionate. As with any other cat, your relationship with your feral cat will be full of opportunities to get to know one another.

The feral cat usually possesses the following traits that

with time, patience, and love can be neutralized so he can live to enjoy a harmonious life:

Feral	*Domesticated*
Fright—The feral cat is driven by fright and easily spooked	*Friendship—As he responds to treatment, familiarity will blossom and fear will slowly be diffused*
Escape—He's always wary of danger and ready to escape at the slightest sudden sound or movement	*Endurance—He will begin to tolerate unpredicted movements instead of resorting to flight*
Routine—A change of routine threatens him because he feels out of control	*Relax—Eventually, he won't be traumatized by a change of routine but will be able to slowly accept it*
Apprehensive—He is instinctively apprehensive and suspicious; to trust may be to fall prey	*Acceptance—Trust will slowly replace suspicion*
Loneliness—To stay apart from humans is his MO, even if there's a part of him that seeks contact	*Love—His desire for human contact wins out*

These innate qualities can be changed to qualities of companionship and, eventually, even intimacy.

ADVANTAGES OF SOCIALIZATION

It is not a piece of cake to tame a feral cat. But you usually don't have to worry about such a cat wreaking havoc with your furnishings. Because he has led such a secretive existence for survival's sake, a feral cat generally stays close to the ground and prefers to be concealed. On the streets his way of life was to stay with the known and familiar. Consequently, he won't be eager to explore new spaces. With an older feral, it may be months or even years before he decides to adorn a cabinet or table. It will probably be rare that you have to say no to your feral cat, because he won't be delinquent.

A feral cat's credo is "curiosity can kill this cat," so you will notice that he is an accurate barometer of people's energy. He is usually wary of those people who are high energy and receptive to those who are not. Even some friends whom you've felt to be calm and easygoing may actually be inwardly tense, and he may distance himself from them because their tension makes him anxious. Similarly, your tension or angst will also cause him to retreat if possible. So when your behavior appears to especially rattle him, stop and think about what may be troubling you. Consider him your perpetual resident therapist. You will find that he will teach you how to keep your life simple. That's quite a gift!

Show Cats and Celebrity Cats

You've been to a few cat shows, and you love to see cats in commercials and advertisements. It occurred to you that one of your cats might be a potential candidate for one or more of these arenas. He adores people and feline company and is most happy when he is front and center. When he's motivated, he even has a few tricks that he performs, and he purrs when he's complimented on his brilliant performance. Your highly sociable cat is a mixed breed, but you know there are cat shows that have Household Divisions, and the media certainly isn't pedigree exclusive. Perhaps you should do some research and see if he could be a show and/or celebrity cat.

CAT SHOWS

The International Cat Show Association (TICA) and Cat Fanciers' Association (CFA) are two of the major producers of cat shows. You can find their events listed in *Cat Fancy* and *Cats* magazines. Shows are worth attending even if you do not plan a career for your cat. These shows have exhibitors with their felines, and there are also many speakers on cat-related topics, educational pamphlets, and various new products, as well as arts and crafts items featuring cats. Many rescue organizations participate, and at the show arrangements can be made for future adoptions.

When you attend the shows, pay attention to what a show cat experiences and talk to some of the care-givers to get an idea of the time and cost commitment necessary to prepare for a show. Perhaps you could enter your cat in a contest as a trial run to see what his reaction is. For this type of competition, he wouldn't have to endure long hours at the show. Most cat shows have a contest that is open to household mixed breeds in which they're judged for many different qualities. Some are quite whimsical, such as a cat-and-person look-alike competition. There may also be a category for shelter-rescued animals.

A cat who is extremely social and mild-mannered may be a natural show cat. Of course, your cat should be in good health, because a show can be very taxing on his health. There are some shows that require veterinary certification prior to entrance to ensure that diseases are not transmitted between cats. Even if the show you enter doesn't require vetting, make sure your cat is healthy and trim his claws. Declawed cats are not eligible for CFA shows.

A cat who becomes overanxious and/or aggressive is probably not cat-show material because he will be surrounded by many cats, a great number of whom are intact. Consequently, the high hormonal level could increase his angst. Why subject your cat to a potentially stress-filled situation if he's apt to be adversely affected?

Preparing for a Show

You'll need to acquaint your cat with the carrier you plan to transport him in. It's important that he's comfortable in it, because he may need to be contained for a while. Play with him in it at home and leave it where he can use it as a retreat. If you plan to enter him in a competition, where he has to be enclosed for long periods of time, you might want to purchase a plastic kennel called a Show Case. The Show Case has been the newest replacement for the traditional cage, and new products are always in the wings. Acquaint him with his new abode before the show so he'll develop a friendly relationship with it.

You can decorate his show abode. Don't forget to bring along a litter box, litter, a supply of food, water, and bowls. Include a couple of his favorite toys and make an audiotape for him to take along for his relaxation. You should record loud noises so he will be desensitized before you reach the show hall (see Chapter 10).

If the show turns out to be a pleasurable experience for both of you, try a repeat performance. Remember, there are cats with champions in their family tree who are not show-cat candidates. So don't be disappointed if your cat goes over the edge. There are those cats that thrive on the excitement, but others are indifferent to the show scene. Don't push your cat if he isn't show-cat material. But if he enjoys the attention and can tolerate the high energy, he may be a natural show cat.

CELEBRITY CATS

You have a people-loving, fun-loving cat who loves to be on camera but goes bonkers when around other cats. He might be appropriate for print or live commercials where he may not have to face other cats. There are agents who

specialize in cats for advertising and there are animal train-
ers who work with cats who are star material. If he has
a high tolerance of new situations, noise, and high-tech
equipment, a celebrity or star role may be his cup of nip.
Your cat and the camera could possibly share a mutual
love affair. A cat can be motivated to perform by food and
attention. But he must usually have a desire to perform a
particular trick. Your wish is not necessarily his command.

When all is said and done, you may decide that you
and your cat would prefer to exhibit his star qualities exclusively in your own home.

Senior Cat

ANTICIPATE YOUR CAT'S GOLDEN YEARS

Your cat will soon be ten, which is the beginning of his senior years. You can ease him into his golden years with the following care:

- Schedule a physical checkup at least twice a year. If there's an existing problem, he may need more medical attention.

- Your cat's teeth should be checked at each exam. Teeth and gum problems are common in older cats. If dentistry is required, a blood test should be done to see if your cat is a good candidate for anesthesia.

- Cooked chicken necks and backs, whose bones are not known to splinter, and dry food will provide good exercise for teeth and gums. You can also consult your veterinarian for specific food suggestions.

- Carbohydrates, such as noodles, creamed food, and rice, are easy on the kidneys and provide a good source of energy. They are easy for the kidneys to break down and utilize unless your cat has a bladder or kidney problem. Your cat might appreciate such a treat—but don't overindulge.

- Add ¼ teaspoon each of brewer's yeast and wheat germ to his food. Do not do this if there is a bladder or kidney malfunction. They're great for stress reduction.

- A urinalysis every few months will indicate the status of his kidney function.

- A slightly chubby cat fares better than a twiggy if he goes off his food for a while.

- Be generous with compliments. Such input will build his self-esteem. The happier he feels, the more he'll relax and the healthier he'll be. Contact is also very important.

- Double up on the hugs and strokes. A senior cat often becomes a lovaholic.

- Encouragement from you can bring out the lover in him.

The average life span of an indoor cat is about fourteen to fifteen years. But some cats have reached their twenties and perhaps a tad more. The more you nurture your cat the more likely he is to live long into his golden years.

MOBILITY

There was a time when your cat was the epitome of speed and spark. But in the past year he's slowed down and appears to be somewhat cautious in his steps. You worry about him and wonder how you can make his days easier.

As a cat matures in years, his mobility isn't as great as before. Don't laugh at his missteps because it will only add to his discomfort and insult his dignity. Instead, tell him how graceful he is and give him a lift with a few hugs.

- Put a stool or bench next to the bed so he doesn't have to exert himself. You might put a stepladder beside a high perch to ease his climb.

- Add a few throw rugs to soften his steps and keep him from slipping if you have bare floors.

- Keep his claws trimmed so they don't impair his movements.

- Curtail his outdoor privileges if there's danger from the great outdoors. It's not unusual for an outdoor cat to become more homebound as he gets on in years. His wanderlust is replaced by dreams and luxurious sleep. If he becomes a couch potato, encourage him to walk about with the aid of one of his toys. Light exercise will enhance his circulation.

SENSES

Your cat's five senses may not be as keen as they used to be. You can help to fill in the blanks.

Sight

Your cat's vision may slowly decline. To help him, try not to redecorate or move furniture. If he's been navigating your house by memory, change could frustrate and disorient him. If you must make changes, slowly walk him around the new additions and repeat to avoid confusion. If your cat's tear ducts become inactive, artificial tears can help lubricate his eyes. Consult his vet for advice.

Hearing

His ears no longer perk up at the slightest noise. Raise your voice when you talk to him. When you approach him, make your movements louder. Because you don't want to startle him, tap on a nearby object so the vibration will announce your appearance. If your cat seems to have lost a substantial percentage of his hearing, a physical checkup is suggested.

Smell

Your foodaholic may become a finicky eater. If so, that can be a signal that he's losing his sense of smell. Add a tad of fishy broth or gravy to his food, or warm his food to tempt him with stronger odors.

Taste

Meals may lack their appeal if your cat's taste buds weaken. Varied menus, special treats, and a taste of your dinner should remedy this. A touch of catnip may also be an effective appetite stimulant.

Touch

Suddenly your cat doesn't like to roughhouse. He almost moans when you pick him up. His favorite high perch is abandoned, and his hallway jaunts are shortened. His limbs are probably less flexible and his all-over pep level has fallen off.

Encourage his circulation with a rubdown or massage. A brushing or combing may also please him. Talk to him all the while. Because heat will soothe his body, fix a cozy nook in the sun or perhaps a safety heating pad that won't overheat. But whatever you do, don't make him feel undignified if you have to carry him to his next destination. Relax your body so he'll do the same. You'll soon be able to anticipate his needs and prevent any stressful activity.

GERIATRIC MALADIES

Indiscriminate Urination

Your cat's litter box habits have always been terrific. But now you find a trickle of urine next to the box once or twice a day. You're puzzled by his new behavior. A kidney malfunction may be the cause of this strange behavior. Schedule an exam to have a urinalysis and bloodwork done. A change of diet may be enough to remedy the situation. If the malfunction is more serious, your cat may need fluid therapy to flush out his kidneys and maintain his hydration. You can do this at home with the proper instructions. But if you aren't willing to do it yourself, you can arrange for someone, probably through the veterinarian's office, to give your cat the necessary fluids.

Indiscriminate urination may also be a sign of diabetes. If that's the case, your cat will probably need daily insulin injections. Don't fear! You'll be able to do this at home and your cat will adjust to the new routine. A special food regimen may also be prescribed.

A cardiac, thyroid, or bladder problem may also trigger indiscriminate urination. A thorough medical exam will reveal the answer.

Leukemia, infectious peritonitis, or feline AIDS is sometimes the cause of puddles outside the box. It's not uncommon for a cat diagnosed with the above maladies to be maintained on medication and tender care.

Indiscriminate Defecation

The other day your cat left a pile on the bathroom mat and yesterday another in the foyer. What could be the matter with him? Indiscriminate defecation can be a result of constipation. A revised diet and medication is often the solution.

Inflammatory bowel syndrome or colitis may cause your cat to have diarrhea. Change of diet and medication can regulate such problems.

Megacolon, or inability to pass stool, could be the cause. This can be alleviated with medication. See your veterinarian.

Impacted anal glands can cause your cat to have deviant defecation habits. The veterinarian can inspect his anal glands and instruct you how to do so in the future.

It's important for you to realize that if your senior cat becomes peculiar in his litter box habits, it's your cue to schedule an appointment with the veterinarian to determine if this behavior is a result of physical illness and how it can be remedied. If your cat's problem is emotional, it may be that your cat needs some special and increased intimate attention (see Chapter 9). His incidents may be a plea for more affection.

Grooming

It astonishes you that your cat's coat looks somewhat shabby. He appears to groom himself less, which is so unlike him. You can fill in for his lack of attention to his appearance.

A vigorous or gentle brushing (his choice) once or twice a day will spruce up his fur and improve his general circulation, which slows with age. Some cats prefer a rubber brush, others a metal comb. Your cat may even enjoy a grooming mitt. Experiment to determine which tool works best.

Mix ¼ teaspoon of brewer's yeast in his food twice a day. If this disagrees with him, ask the vet to recommend a supplement that's high in B vitamins. These are good for the coat and also reduce stress. The veterinarian may also want to adjust your cat's diet.

A supplement called Gold Caps may be purchased at your local pet supply shop (or call 800-783-0977).

A humidifier will add moisture to the atmosphere, which will enhance his fur.

Excessive Grooming

Lately your cat has become an obsessive groomer. His stomach has become his target, and it is almost bare. This puzzles you!

This obsessiveness may be the result of an underlying medical problem that needs immediate attention, such as a cardiac problem, asthma, epilepsy, or an allergy to something in his environment, such as rugs, cleaning agents, or plants.

Diet may play a part in this behavior. Perhaps there's a deficiency or an allergy to food.

Emotional stress is often the cause of excessive grooming. A cat fixates on a certain area of his body and licks away when he becomes frustrated or anxious. Spend extra quality time with your cat. If your schedule is too frantic, arrange for a friend or professional cat sitter to be a surrogate you. You might want to make his own audiocassette to relax him. The more relaxed he is, the less he'll groom. Leave him messages on your answering machine. He should be soothed by your voice. Generally an injectable or oral anti-inflammatory medication from the veterinarian should relieve the discomfort caused by his excessive grooming. If the problem continues despite your best efforts, you might want to engage a cat therapist to provide specialized help.

Asthma

The other night your cat interrupted your deep slumber with a few coughs. The next morning his breathing was irregular. It may be your cat has a slight case of asthma and needs medication to remedy this distress. See your veterinarian. An air cleaner would help to make his respiration easier. Also try to keep smokers away from him. Remove any of his toys that may cause him to cough or become uncomfortable.

Although asthma can generally be controlled with proper medication and precautions, regular thorough dusting and vacuuming will help to remove irritating particles that can affect your cat's respiration. Carpets and furniture can be treated with a spray that contains tannic acid. This temporarily neutralizes pollen and house dust allergens. Sometimes a chiropractor can offer relief.

Nocturnal Angst

Your cat has always been a solid gold sleeper, as have you. But for the last few weeks about an hour after you're both settled in bed, he starts to cry, and the cry gets louder and louder. Sometimes he runs around and cries. Cuddles, soft words, and food do nothing to stop his hysteria, and if you put him in another room, you still get no peace.

Your cat's nocturnal angst may be a result of thyroid or other type of medical problem. Schedule a physical exam.

This behavior could also be a result of anxiety caused by a change in your schedule or a major loss of a person or feline companion. Sometimes your cat can be sensitive to your biological rhythm, which changes during the night and especially as your waking time approaches. Arrange to give your cat a vigorous workout each evening to release his pent-up energy. If the racket still persists, sequester him in a small room with his creature comforts and soft radio music to soothe him. You can each have your separate boudoirs. Be sure to do this with affection and not anger. (See also pages 146–150.)

COMPANIONS AND LOSS

A New Companion

Your cat's companion of twelve years met his demise two weeks ago. It was sudden. At first your cat appeared confused, but otherwise he appears to be himself. Maybe he's a tad more affectionate. You're not sure if a new companion would make him happy or disappoint him. His late companion was always the leader and top cat.

If your cat appears to be in good spirits after the demise of his companion, it may be that he prefers the role of a single cat and exclusive attention. Let things be and see if this attitude is sustained. If your cat becomes morose, cries for no apparent reason, picks at or inhales his food, or panics when you're out of his sight, this is probably his appeal for a new companion. Generally, it's easier to introduce a kitten. If your cat is very athletic, choose a very playful kitten. A more sedate kitten would be best if your cat has a subdued catsonality. An adolescent or mature cat may be an appropriate companion if he has a mellow and cat-oriented nature so he will instinctively seek out the companionship of your cat. It would be best to have a neutral party escort the newcomer in to your home so your cat does not feel betrayed. (Refer to Chapter 8.) If your cat has had a traumatic incident with a cat of a particular color, avoid that color of cat. A cat can detect color by its scent. If your cat had a loving bond with his previous companion, opt for a new companion of the same sex as your cat's departed friend.

One-cat Household—Your Choice

Your lifestyle won't allow you to acquire a new companion for your cat, but there must be ways to improve his quality of life.

- Arrange for a neighbor, responsible child, or professional cat sitter to make daily visits—or at least when you're especially detained.

- Perhaps a couple of tropical fish in a cat-proof tank would entertain him.

- Leave him messages on your answering machine so he can hear your voice. He'll relax to your familiar voice. Be sure to praise him frequently.

- You might be able to arrange play dates if there's a cat or dog nearby with whom he's compatible.

One-cat Household—Your Cat's Preference

Three months have gone by since the demise of your beloved cat. Your surviving cat appears to be very contented with his role of single cat. But you are distraught! You'd love to have another cat. You miss the affection of two cats and the joy of their interaction with each other. What should you do?

- You could adopt a feral or especially cat-oriented young kitten or adolescent. This wouldn't give you another cat to immediately love. But perhaps in time, the cat would turn to you for attention. It would avoid an upset of your senior cat's peace of mind.

- Volunteer work at a nearby shelter or veterinary hospital would provide you with interaction from cats and dogs who are most needy and grateful for attention.

- Cat sit for friends' cats. You might even decide to set up a small cat-sitting service.

- Be good to yourself and nurture your mind, body and spirit with things that enrich you. Your cat will reap the benefits, too.

Resident or Mascot Cats

This is a list of the cats that I have met and worked with throughout my years of practice. This list may be incomplete, so I'm thankful for the cat's exquisite gift of forgiveness.

Veterinary Hospitals

Westside Veterinary Center (Manhattan)
    Mr. C., Willie
Animal Clinic of New York (Manhattan)
    Beau, Jack Gump, Michael J.
Animal General (Manhattan)
    Katie
Ansonia Veterinary Center (Manhattan)
    Butch
The Cat Practice (Manhattan)
    Beat

Center for Veterinary Care (Manhattan)
    Kitty
Dr. Thomas De Vincentis
    Burl
Cobble Hill Animal Hospital (Brooklyn)
    Sunny
Feline Health (Manhattan)
    Basil
Feline Veterinary Hospital (Pt. Washington)
    Spice, Gran Ma
Forest Hills Cat Hospital (Glendale, Queens)
    Blackie, Boots
Just Cats (Pt. Jefferson)
    Edgar, Moses
Dr. Mary Lee Keating
    Cleo, Lucky
American Animal Hospital (Mt. Freedom, N.J.)
    Lucy
Park East Animal Hospital (Manhattan)
    Lulu, Tuesday
St. Marks Veterinary Hospital (Manhattan)
    Sebastian
Washington Square Animal Hospital (Manhattan)
    Angela
Clinique Veterinaire (Montréal)
    Peanuts, Mr. Gray
    (Guests for the day)
Chats Décarie Veterinary Clinic (Montréal)
    Pushkin (guest)

Shops

    Barking Zoo (Manhattan)
        Amelia
    Beasty Feast (Manhattan)
        Zoro

Creature Features (Manhattan)
    Nekko
Kat Sou (Montréal)
    Frosty
Maxine Bailey (Montréal)
    Charlie
Pet Stop (Manhattan)
    Monkey, Rose Bud
Whiskers (Manhattan)
    Pretty
Beekman Pet Emporium (Manhattan)
    Minnie, Arthur
Mimi Varg Olsen, Pet Portrait Painter
    Onyx, Bushy, Hedy

Index